GREETINGS FROM THE OTHER SIDE:
WELCOME TO YOUR NEW BUSINESS (AD)VENTURE?

By Scott M. Annes

This book his humbly dedicated to the many, many people that I have had the honor to know and sometimes work with in running their businesses over these past many years. You have all taught me so much.

It is, as always, also dedicated to my family and friends and especially to Susan and the boys. Thanks for letting me stay up late and helping me to wake up early.

And it is dedicated to the memory of John "Tiny" Konrad who single handedly shared more wisdom with me than I could ever have acquired in ten live times. I hope that you were proud of me Tiny.

Another Foreword: Deja-New

Greetings from the other side. You have made it. You have gone into business for yourself and you are certain that you are on the road to success. You have quit buying lottery tickets and you have stopped praying. Success is just waiting to walk through the door of your small enterprise. And you are waiting for it. And you are WAITING for it . . . Here it comes, your success, it's right outside the door. Still waiting . . . . .and waiting and waiting . . . . and waiting.

As you are waiting, you say to yourself, Do you know what? Success has always procrastinated when it came to visiting me so now I am committed to the personal satisfaction that I feel from opening my small business. Here I am I am waiting for satisfaction. It's just outside my front door, I know it. Here it comes. Still waiting. . .and waiting. I am just going to go the bathroom for a few minutes. Satisfaction you come in when you're ready. . . . I'm still waiting . . And waiting.

Well here you are without success and satisfaction. They are both in the hallway outside the office having a laugh and you are diligently sitting at your desk that you bought on credit. You have eight cartons of staples including the free one that came with that electric stapler you had to have and you have not yet stapled a single staple. The mailman will be dropping off that credit card bill in a few minutes. You could staple that to your head so that it is there every time you look in the mirror.

Some of you might now be thinking: I have encountered this tone from a writer before. This foreword reminds me of another one that I read. The writer of that book thought it was funny to turn opening your own business into a satire of sorts. With the use of sarcasm and appreciation for sadism, he extolled the lack of virtue and the shear ignorance it takes to open your own business. He made fun of everything. He made fun of himself. He made fun of me!

But that book was about opening a new business. If you are reading this, or if you just picked it up, you are passed opening your new business. If you are reading this book then you have probably already committed to the insane notion that you can operate a successful small business. Heck, you are already running it. You were looking to this book for some sage advice on how to continue with your quest. You are well passed starting the quest.

If you went ahead and opened your business, then hopefully, you have read the outstanding book "Who Wants to be a Businessaire?" The author's name escapes me but I was impressed by his work just the same. If you read that book, then you recognize that unmistakable tone in this book. More importantly, if you read that book and it made you think and it made you laugh, even at yourself, then you have one of the prerequisites to succeed as you continue in business. You have the ability to not take yourself too seriously.

This book has some similarities to its predecessor. As you read it you will get the same feel and it will seem familiar but it will be different. I call this concept, Deja-New. It feels like we have been here before but we are sure this is new territory. It is like having a point of reference in a completely new experience. What you read in this book will build on what you might recall from the past. However, if you did not read the other book or you do not recall much, do not worry. The intention of this foreword is to reacquaint you with the feel we developed in the previous book.

So think of this foreword as you would the opening scene in *Star Wars* where several paragraphs of yellow letters scroll past you against the back drop of deep space and Mr. Lucas tells you what has happened in the story and where you are at now. You got the image? Good. Here we go.

In our last episode, the poor fool of a hero to our story was trying to open his or her own business while dealing with numerous decisions, obstacles, red tape, general worry and in some cases panic. The Empire had chased our small business owner away with so many details that our poor owner had no idea what to do. Feeling overwhelmed, poor owner read, "Who Wants to be a Businessaire?" and thought that maybe it would help with the decisions and the obstacles and the head-aches. But our hero learned that that book was all about what it "feels" like to be in business. There was some practical advice but for the most part, it was a book full of wise-ass comments and stupid anecdotes about what you will face if you open your own business. Nevertheless, the Empire was thwarted by our hero's reliance upon that book. That magical book helped our hero escape the challenges put in his or her way by the Empire and our hero got the business off the ground.

Now, having escaped the obstacles to opening a new business with the help of that magical book, our hero now faces all sorts of new challenges. As our hero runs the business, our hero begins to experience all sorts of emotions from malaise to complacency. Our hero is distraught some days and merely anxious on others. Escaping the Empire and starting a new business was not merely enough for our hero. Now our hero seeks success. And the book he had cannot get our hero to where our hero needs to go.

Meanwhile, the Empire awaits our hero's first big misstep. Will he or she lose a client, lose a source of supply, lose an employee, or just lose their mind? Should any of this happen, our hero is alone armed only with a new book of secrets to face the Empire as it prepares to pounce. The new book of secrets, code named: GFTOS, is reminiscent of what our hero enjoyed about the other book. But where the old book dealt with the feel of opening and being in business, the new book of secrets will help our hero to develop a feel for what it is like to cope as our hero continues in business.

Just picture those three paragraphs being scrolled across the screen in bright yellow letters with outer space in the background.

Okay, now leave the theater and come with me. We are going on a trip through the everyday annoyances of continuing in that business I attempted to persuade you not to open with the book "Who Wants to Be a Businessaire?" Now that you are in business, I would like to entreat you to try some of the techniques used in this book to develop a feel for what it is to commit to the business you have already started. You have gone ahead and got the boat out of the harbor but now how do you sail it on the seas? This book is all about what you face on the seas. It is not so much a "how to" as it is a "what's this?" In order to deal with what you will encounter as you sail out into the sea, this book addresses what it "feels" like to overcome things and prepare for things you will face in business.

Once again I will infuse anecdotes and commentary to drive home some points. I like humor, so I will use that too. I like to laugh at what I wrote. You may also laugh at what I wrote so long as you pay for the opportunity to read it. That also makes me laugh as I think about how I wrote something stupid that I thought was funny and then you paid me money to read it and maybe think it was funny. Forgive my condescension, but that is funny.

So what does "Greeting from the other Side?" mean? Well I have observed over the years that there are two types of people in the world when it comes to opening a new business. There are the "thinking about it" folks and the doers. I have encountered a great many "thinking about it" folks. They typically have times when it is a better idea than at other times. For example, when their employment gets crappy or when their boss dumps on them, then opening their own business does not seem so bad. These people usually find an excuse that prevents them from finally pulling the trigger and starting out on their own however. Some of those reasons are good ones (e.g. "I have a family to support"), some are not so good ("I have no idea how I would get it started, there seems to be no books about opening a new business"). Some of these folks are too lazy and some are too scared.

But to those of you who overcame the reasons not to and overcame the nagging excuses in your way and overcame your fear and overcame any lack of ambition you might have harbored, I salute you. You have made it to the other side. So, may I say it again, Greeting from the other Side!

Back when you were one of those "thinking about it" folks, you had plenty of "how to" books. Now that you are over here unfortunately, you may find that there are not many books to tell you how to keep going with something you have already started. For those of you looking for a book to help you through those really crappy days you encounter while running your business, here it is. Your book has arrived. I am all too happy to help. For those of you who bought this book for someone else, I thank you. For those of you who have read it and then gave it to someone else, well thanks a lot. I get nothing from you loaning it to someone else. Nothing, diddly, zero, zip, nadda. If you are reading this and you got it for nothing all I can say is send the cover price to my publisher. Do not send cash. Who knows if I will ever see a penny of that. Send a check. Make it payable to me and my publisher. That way they will have to call me to indorse it and I will at least see some of the money. Thanks.

What will this book be like? The book will not always seem intelligent because I am not that bright. I observe people and business owners as part of my work. So, this book has insight developed from my observations of people who struggle with all sorts of problems. One of the problems that we deal with is success. The book provides insight on how some people struggle with success. We will point out how "struggling with success" is not as much of an oxymoron as you might think.

Perhaps it would be easier for me to state what I would like for the reader to get from this book as opposed to what the book will be like. What I would like for the reader to gain from this book is the most important thing any small business owner needs. What this book is ultimately about is perspective. Your ability to put things into and then maintain perspective is what continuing in your small business is all about. Without taking yourself too seriously and with a genuine ability to be objective and honest with yourself, you might find this book helpful. Maybe, you will even conquer the Empire. Maybe, it will help you to be a hero.

PART I
MANAGING THINGS LIKE TIME, STRESS and FRUSTRATION

CHAPTER 1
Culpability for your situation, you got yourself into this, now . . .

I have a saying. It goes like this. Working sucks and when you work for yourself, you have yourself to blame. So does that mean if I did not work for myself, it would suck less. Maybe, maybe not. If you worked for someone else, you would blame them for your life being miserable. If your employees' lives suck, some of them probably blame you.

What make working suck? There are a lot of things I could point to but the major one is stress. Face it, it is stressful to have to always have to put your effort into your work. You have to think during work. You have to execute. You have to please people. You have to please people on days when you do not give a damn about them. You have to convince people that you like them when they are driving you nuts. How could that not suck?

Sometimes you have to please a great many people. Sometimes you have to please a great many people who, no matter how hard you try, cannot be pleased. Working makes you do what you usually do not want to do.

Now I know there are exceptions. There are always exceptions. But, for the most part, working results in stress and stress sucks. Does everything stressful suck? Sex can be stressful and for most people they still engage in it. Roller coasters cause stress and yet people still ride. Sure, there is a difference between the stress you feel from the exhilaration of sex or a roller coaster. (How about sex on a roller coaster? Now that would be stressful! Do not write in, I am sure some of you have done it. Do not tell me about it. I could only be jealous. There. Feel better?)

Anyway, just as there are different types of stress, there are different ways in which working sucks. Sometimes it sucks because you have too much to do. Sometimes it sucks because you do not have enough to do. Sometimes it sucks because you are expected to do something that you cannot reasonably do. Sometimes it sucks because it is boring or not challenging enough. For your part, all you know is that working sucks more times than not having to work.

For the most part, working sucks because so much of it involves problem solving. The phrase 'problem solving" necessarily implies bad stuff because it involves "problems" which are bad and "solving" which implies hard work. No one likes problems. Even if they are somewhat challenging, problems are not what anyone strives to endure. Many people try to avoid problems or ignore problems or simply run away from their problems. Worse yet, many people try to avoid the work that actually solves problems. This goes to the heart of why working sucks. It sucks to have problems and it sucks to have to exert effort and time to solve them. No matter how you look at it though, problems need to be resolved and work is what it takes to resolve problems.

The difference between the stress that anyone working for someone else and what the entrepreneur feels is that when you work for someone else, money problems are not what is stressful. If you work for someone else, other than maybe an airline or American automaker, you usually do not worry about the company's ability to pay you. But, if you are the head honcho and it is your business, you have to worry about paying everyone else and then yourself. This is one of your problems to solve along with all the others. On top of all that sucks about having to work, when you add that pressure to make and get money to it, working for yourself sucks worse.

And who do you have to thank for leading you to that point in your life where you just had to be the boss? In business for yourself, you can blame yourself. Without someone to scapegoat for you being in this stressful situation, that adds to the stress as you have no outlet with which to release your frustration.

I have seen many entrepreneurs try to release their frustration in these situations. They start talking to themselves in the third person. "Damn it Scott, what were you thinking? You idiot Scott, you have really put me behind the 8-ball! Writing this book is such a pain in the ass Scott, just like you. For Christ's sakes, Scott, you ask way too much of me!" All of this is said, looking in a mirror.

Do you know how to kill that third person? Do something great in your business and they magically disappear. "Wow, I did do a great job, didn't I? I have to admit that I am pretty proud of myself. Sure I pulled it off. Lesser people would not have been able to but I did it! I really had to push myself, but this book was worth it."

Being in business for yourself, as you have learned from experience, is stressful for a myriad of reasons. Avoiding that stress is impossible. There simply are too many reasons to be stressful. Usually, it is a matter of trying to make a living for yourself and your employees while also juggling keeping customers happy, paying your creditors and sending your Uncle Sam a cut. That may seem to be an oversimplification of it to many but that is really all it is about. In my opinion, the one thing that eliminates much of the stress is simplifying things and in some cases, oversimplifying things.

I came to the conclusion a long time ago as I observed that much of my clients' stress came from complication and complexity. They would never be handling just one problem at a time. They would be handling a great many problems and one would overlap onto the other and, before long, everything was stressful. When your life is complicated and unnecessarily complex then, even the small stuff is stressful.

We have all heard the phrase, he could not tell the forest from the trees. That sometimes applies to the small business owner. Sometimes they get so far into the woods that all they see is the darkness caused by the bunching of all the trees. If they could step outside themselves for a moment, however, they might be able to look at the entire forest from the outside and they might be able to figure out a way to get themselves out from the darkness.

I am not going to start preaching about perspective at this point. Do not worry, I will get plenty preachy about perspective throughout the book but this is intended to be the first chapter. I am giving you a break. For now.

Without approaching your problems by assessing your perspective, you need to do something else. You need to simplify things. Assess your ultimate goal. If it is to make money, then find the easiest way to do that. If it is to increase market share, just do it. If it is to raise customer satisfaction, then raise customer satisfaction.

If that goal is blocked by obstacles, assess what is the biggest obstacle and face it. Do not merely face the small obstacles and avoid the big ones. Face the big ones and achieve your goals.

One of the best methods to simplify your life is to avoid abstractions. Render all of your problems to only one plane as opposed to three or more dimensions. If your thinking is not too complicated then your problem solving will be more fluid and potentially more efficient.

Try this. Think of everything in your business as being on a single plane like a white sheet of paper. On a single plane, everything is a matter of geography. Now write your name on the top of the paper. Then, write your goal at the bottom of the paper. Write down your biggest obstacle in the middle of the paper. Now, just think of a way to get rid of whatever is in between you and your goals.

I am not mocking anyone with this exercise. Try it. Ask yourself, do I have the creativity to overcome the simple geographic dilemma posed by this exercise? You should recognize that your creativity is what gets you through the problems and stress you feel in your business. So how do you handle this exercise?

Do you have scissors? Well then go ahead and cut the middle out of the paper. Problem solved - goal achieved. Do you have a pen? Scratch out the middle of the paper. Problem solved - goal achieved. No pen and no scissor. Do you have a brain? Fold the paper in the middle. Problem solved - goal achieved. All three of those methods resulted in you either getting closer to the goal or eliminating what was between you and your goal. This is usually the point where many in the class take their papers, wad them up and throw them at me.

But, the point is clear and most take that away from this exercise. Before you start on yourself about how stressful it is to be in your own business and before you blame yourself, recognize that working sucks, think about what work really is. It is mostly just problem solving. In business for yourself, it is problem solving with the additional pressure of needing to make money. If you can, get rid of all of the complications, focus on the simple aspect of what you need to do to solve the problem and rely upon your creativity. Then you can overcome the stress that you caused for yourself when you decided to go into business. If you do not stop to blame yourself then maybe, just maybe, simplifying your situation will help you gain, dare I say it, the perspective, to handle the stress. After all, what is so stressful about folding a piece of paper.

CHAPTER 2
Everyone who has felt regret over their inability to be better at time management raise your hand. Oh raise your hand for gosh sakes. No one ever feels that they manage time perfectly.

Much like the weather, we all here about "Time Management" but no one ever seems to do anything about it. The thing I think most people dread about the terms "time management" is that they perceive that it requires an element of discipline beyond what anyone can actually do. At that juncture, I advise people to look at things from a purely economic point of view. Economics is the study of how we distribute limited resources amongst individuals with unlimited needs and wants. When thinking of time management we have to consider time itself as a limited resource that we need to utilize in the most efficient manner. We ask the economic questions. What is the actual limit of time? Can we create more time? How can we use the limited time we have to maximize its value?

As with any economic concept, we also need to look at various factors to be considered in our economic decisions. Certain factors require more attention than others. For example, per unit costs might be the factor that one company focuses on while fixed costs might be the factor that another company focuses on. The factors you need to focus on in considering time management are deadlines and time limitations. Notice that each of these factors relate to thoughts about the future. Effective time managers do not obsess about how much time has been lost. They do not obsess about what might have been accomplished. Basically, they do not obsess about the past. Effective time managers do obsess over deadlines however. A deadline is something that is in the prospective rather than bygone. They do not consider their failures but they think about what lies ahead. Effective time managers are focused on what they can get done between now and some point in the future and they do not spend time regretting what they did not get done before now.

Effective time managers also know that feeling guilty about having wasted time in the past is of no consequence. Guilt over things you have already done, or failed to do, is of little importance. Guilt does have some value however. Feeling guilty about something that you are about to do is very productive. This is true especially in the context of time management. If you can force yourself to feel guilty before you intentionally take that two hour lunch, then the guilt may prevent you from doing it in the first place. You should feel guilty about even thinking about wasting time. Guilt over something that you are about to do is the only valuable guilt that there is.

Effective time management also requires some realistic assessment of your particular role in your business. For that we turn to another way of thinking about time.

At one time people said "time is money." For now, let's think of time as gasoline.

Think of time as gasoline. Think of yourself as a car. Now accept the fact that some cars get better mileage than others. Ergo, some people are better time managers than others. So, if I happen to be a car that does not get good gas mileage, how can I compete with cars that get better gas mileage?

Well, think about different types of cars. Cars that can carry more people, like SUV's, have poorer gas mileage. Two seater hybrids get terrific gas mileage. Just like people who deal with lots of people during the day usually have little or no time on their hands. While people who work in a cubical without outside distractions from others have the opportunity to get a great deal accomplished in less time, you have to ask yourself what type of car you are in order to properly assess what type of time mileage you can get out of your day.

As a car, we need to also think about the types of trips we need to take. Most if not all cars get better gas mileage on the highway than in the city. The same is true for people trying to use time better. We generally get more done when we have an uninterrupted period of time to perform tasks. Meanwhile, when we have numerous distractions, our time mileage goes down considerably. Ask yourself about what type of driving you do as a car. Do you make frequent stops? Do you get to drive on the highway? Highway gas mileage is usually better. The difference is whether you get to work straight through an assignment or do you have to accomplish a great many small tasks. All of these differences affect gas mileage. All of these things affect time management.

The point is that you may not be a bad time manager given the type of work you have to do. You might have to deal with new matters and issues as you try to complete routine tasks. In cases like that, your day is anything but routine.

It is hard to manage time when your work is always throwing curve balls at you. So as to take the analogies way too far, remember that you can foul away as many curve balls as you wish but you cannot strike out until you miss one. What I mean is that if your day always throws you curve balls, you do not always have to handle each one perfectly. Perfection, by its very nature implies that you have sufficient time to attain perfection at some task. So you do not have to hit each curve ball out of the park. You can give them as much time as you are able and no more. Maybe you will not handle each one perfectly but you will keep them from counting against you so long as you deal with each one. Check with Major League Baseball. They do not keep records of how many pitches a guy fouled away in all of his at bats. The statistic is not important. So when you are always being thrown lots of little assignments that break up your time management, handle them, do not strive for perfection and by all means, get them out of the way.

Back to our analogy regarding a gas powered car. Some writers use mixed metaphors. Not me however. I use mixed analogies. If you have a lot of small or short trips that will affect your overall gas mileage, cluster them. Take them in an order that makes sense and is efficient. When you have a great many short trips to make you do not return home after each trip. Instead, you leave home and you make stops in groups. Usually, you make groups of stops that are all in the same direction and/or proximity. You hit the grocery store, the gas station and the post office all in the same direction. You might hit the cleaners, the library and the kids' school as stops that are together in the same general area and direction.

Likewise, in order to manage time across a number of small tasks, you can perform similar tasks, if not simultaneously, then in groups. In my office, for example, I return all non emergency calls at a set time during the day. Phone calls can be distracting. So, in order to deal with them, I handle them one after another at a given time during the day. I set parameters for my phone time and then I set parameters for each call. If I have two cases that are similar and I need to do something on each at the same time, I deal with them one right after the other. That way, I take the experiences and knowledge I gain from one and carry it over immediately to the second one. I do not have to waste time remembering how I dealt with the situation last time. I merely do it again after I just did it.

Now for all the analogies and advice regarding time management, the important thing to remember is that you must make the most of the time that you have. This seems simple enough but a lot of business people miss this point. Sometimes, people calculate the amount of time they need to do a job. If they finish it before the calculated time then they waste the time saved patting themselves on the back. This is not making the most of the time you have. Finish early and start the next thing. Acknowledge that there are time limitations to everything including your work day. So, if you get a chance to get ahead on something then do it. Then finish your work day on time and go spend some time with your kids. Remember that time usually works against you. If it forgets itself and leaves some extra time on your plate, then take advantage. Time is usually too stingy to lose itself to you too often.

Another concept to wrap your thinking around is convincing yourself that the time you spend to think of a short cut usually never justifies the short cut. Some people are obsessed with short cuts. As a result, they devote all of their time to finding that elusive "better way" to do something that requires less work and effort than the conventional method. On rare occasions, they come up with a viable way of doing something with less time or effort but the limited frequency of such occasions hardly justifies always looking for shortcuts. The best way to get something done is to do it. The best way to do it is to start to do it. Maybe, if you at least start to do something, the shortcut will occur to you after you begin doing it. In which case, you will not have wasted time just thinking. Think about it.

Time Management Strategies

For those of you who jumped to this section, shame on you. What are you doing? Are you trying to save time or something? Are you so obsessed with time that you do not want to read all the prior fluff in this chapter? Well excuse me if I wasted your time. It probably took me more time to write it than it did for you to have at least skimmed it. So skim it. Okay? It provides context for what is to come.

For the rest of you, after you read this entirely excessively long chapter about managing your time, you ask the question: what specific things can I do to become a better time manager?

The first thing you need to do is assess what you can accomplish. To do this, set realistic goals. Experience will dictate how long it takes to do things. Otherwise guess. Then perform the tasks you need to perform in the time allotted. Do not always run over the time you have allotted. Based on experience, if it took you three hours to balance the checkbook this month it will probably take three hours next month. Three hours is the time you plan on completing that task.

Then, factor in the intangibles. If your work has numerous distractions, factor in time for distractions. If you need to always deal with last minute emergencies, factor time in for those as well. If completing your job is dependent upon someone else completing a corresponding task, then learn how long it takes for them to complete their task. See what you can do to control the amount of time they might take. Otherwise, merely factor in time for them to fail to get their job done on time.

Also, delegate tasks that can be done by others to others who might have more time than you do. For example, if you have to deal with a great many people during the day, then you have to delegate routine time intensive tasks to other people. As you have to employ additional people you have to charge more for the time you spend with people. This is why services cost so much in our society. You see a doctor for ten minutes and get a bill for $175.00. But, you do not see the hours of additional time the doctor's staff has put into charting, recording, billing, booking tee times and following up with you. Your doctor might see 50 patients in a day and might be running late for all but the first one. It seems that his time mileage is low. But, he can compensate by having a staff that does not deal with people as much get more done behind the scenes.

Finally, you need to think about when you are the most productive. Some people are more productive in the morning. Some are more productive when they are under pressure. Some are more productive only when they have a clear goal. For example, I greatly enjoy a casual round of golf and I could take up to five hours to play eighteen holes. But, if you

17

were to tell me on the second hole that it was going to rain within the next hour and that the club house will not refund my greens fee for the round, I could finish eighteen holes in forty-five minutes. This somehow motivates me.

The One Technique that you need to Handle Time Management Issues

One of the best techniques I know of to become better at handling time management issues is actually very simple to think about and reasonably simple to implement. When you have a great deal to do in a limited amount of time you need to develop momentum. That is it. It is no big secret but it is effective.

Now notice I did not say when time is short but I said that time was limited. There is a subtle difference. To say that "time is short" implies that you have more to do than can be done in the amount of time you have. When that is the case, you have to prioritize what things you will not be able to accomplish versus what must be accomplished and you then perform tasks in order.

When "time is limited" however, you have enough time to do all the things that must be done but you have no time to spare. In cases like this developing momentum in attacking your tasks can get you through.

The tricks to developing momentum are fairly uniform. The first is to start early. Do you remember family vacations as a kid? Your father would make sure that you got going as early in the day as possible so as to keep moving. That is the idea behind starting early. To develop momentum, you need to start the initial movement as soon as possible. Without wasting time at the very beginning of a project you will find that it is easier to finish the project.

Now let's face it. At the beginning of any project or any day of work, we all tend to feel that we have all day to finish what we need to finish. At 8:00 AM or even 8:30, what is the big hurry? We have all day. By 12:00 PM when you really have nothing done yet, you start to feel uneasy because you realize that you have wasted time. Maybe you could have finished early if you had only gotten off to a good start but then you console yourself and convince yourself that you can get it done: after lunch. Do not forget that both of the words "console" and "convince" contain the word "con." You have conned yourself. So you go to a longer lunch than you anticipated and you get back around 2:00 PM. Now you feel more than uneasy. You have wasted as much as five hours of the day and now work that builds up during the day has put you even farther behind. If only you had started earlier.

Remember those family vacations you took as a kid. You were mad at your father back then for waking you at 4:30 AM to get on the road. Of course now, as you think back about it, you appreciate what your father had taught you. You could call him to thank him but, you convince yourself that he would have no idea what you are talking about.

Back to our family vacation analogy. What was the other reason your father had for starting early? You remember. Think about it. He wanted to avoid traffic from the early morning rush hour. In the same way, to develop momentum, you need to avoid the early morning delays and distractions that cut into your time. Unless your most important task is to answer e-mails, you do not need to do that first thing. Opening your browser leads to distractions as you peruse the news and scores etc. Frankly, you do not have to do anything that can be a distraction or a diversion.

In addition, do not let your momentum get derailed by obstacles. Deal with the obstacles and keep going. When you hit traffic or detours on your family vacation, you did not stop. You stayed with it and your dad drove and maneuvered through the traffic as quickly as possible. These obstacles slowed momentum but they did not stop the trip. You still made it to Disneyland. Once your dad had the opportunity on the open road again, he drove fast enough to make up for lost time and regained momentum. You were just mad because you had to hold it for two hours while dad promised to pull over at rest stop where he never seemed to have seen the ramp on time. "That's okay Junior, we'll hit the next one. Just hold on."

Distractions having been avoided and obstacles having been overcome, you may now move on to prioritizing tasks. Obviously, you need to do what has to be done. So if a matter is a priority or has a deadline, it is the first thing that you do. But, what if you have many tasks that are a priority or none which are a priority? Well if all things are equal, then you need to move to the next stage in building momentum. That stage entails estimating the time necessary to accomplish each specific tasks.

Then, fit the estimate of time into your day as it is scheduled.

For example, if you have ten letters to write to clients and you estimate that it will take you two hours to write all of them, you are ready to schedule the first two hours of your day. Perhaps, you need to do some other task first however and you usually leave for lunch at 1:00 PM. If that is the case, move the two hour project to 11:00 AM. and let yourself know that you will not leave for lunch until all the letters are out. Set a goal of finishing the other project that you have before 11:00 AM and you have now scheduled your morning. Get everything done that you planned to before lunch and that will set you in a better mind set for accomplishing things after lunch. Also, for purposes of building momentum, getting done what you set out to get done assures that you do not fall behind. Falling behind kills momentum. So now, as you leave for lunch at 1:00 to 1:15 PM, you have accomplished what you set out to do that morning and you have convinced yourself that you can do it. That also builds momentum.

The trick now is to get back to work as soon as you get back from lunch. If lunch is too much of a distraction, eat at your desk and keep moving. The best thing to do to build momentum is to keep moving and to, at all costs, avoid stops that will kill momentum. Once momentum is going, it is self sustaining. It usually keeps going until some outside force stops it. Restarting anything takes time and never goes as smoothly as we would like. It takes thought to restart something. The thought process leads to distraction. Distraction kills momentum. Remember your father on those family vacations. Stops were avoided. If he could have put a toilet in the back seat and refilled up for gas by syphoning off a moving gas tanker, he would have. Your father knew the value of momentum. He got you to your vacation spot by strictly making sure that you kept moving.

Momentum also comes from finishing a great many tasks before tackling the larger things on your to do list. Our ability to concentrate for lengthy periods of time is limited. Concentrating on smaller tasks requires less effort and is less taxing on our ability to build momentum. You build momentum and confidence by saying that you got ten of the fifteen things you needed to get done before lunch done. If you only finish one big assignment however, you still have fourteen other things to do to get caught up. The other problem is that in thinking about the time you will consume on bigger projects, you can become overwhelmed. This also kills momentum. So, unless it is a priority, get the small stuff done and move on to the larger stuff last.

Once you get moving and accomplish one or two things, do not stop. Do not take a break to pat yourself on the back. This breaks the momentum that you have achieved thus far. Do not take a detour, do not pass go, do not collect $200.00. Go directly to the next task. But I am proud of myself. I need recognition. My answer is do more and be more proud at the end of the day when you have done all that you set out to do.

This brings us to a very important point about momentum. It requires discipline. If you did not have some degree of discipline, then you would never have opened your own business. So now, as you try to accomplish more with each business day, use the discipline that is innate in each of you who have undertaken to become entrepreneurs.

What will happen eventually as you implement the technique of developing momentum is that you will move from the type of person who is proud of himself or herself for each task performed and more proud of the totality of work performed in a day. You could be the type of person who says: "How great is this? I got that big project done by 4:00 and left early." Or you could be the guy or girl who says: "What a productive day. I finished the big project and still had three hours to get some of the other things that had to be done out of the way. At this rate, by 5:00 on Friday, I will have gotten my entire desk cleaned off from everything that had been building up on it!"

You know the difference between these two types of people when you see them leave for vacation. One is working until midnight to be able to go away and still leaves a desk full of work that will only build up while she or he is away. Meanwhile the latter leaves at 5:00 with a perfectly organized desk and nothing left to be done. Disciplined people leave for vacation with a clean desk and a cleaner conscience. They get home on time the night before their vacation and they pack efficiently. They get to bed early and have a good night sleep. Then, they leave for their vacation early in the morning to get going and avoid traffic just like their fathers taught them.

CHAPTER 3
Manage Stressment, Stressment Management, Management Stress and Stress Management

I have an adage that I believe that I created. I came up with it when I was in rehab. (Don't tell Oprah but the truth is, I was never in rehab. My only addiction is to golf and I am a 9 handicap - Don't tell that to Oprah either because I don't want her to tell Larry King that it was in the spirit of being a 9 handicap that caused me to say that in my book despite the fact that I am actually an 18 handicap. I do not want my enthusiastic embellishments to land me on Oprah's couch from where she throws me under a bus for lying in my book that she just had to have in her book club. But I digress.).

My personal adage is simple:

I cannot solve all of my problems today but, I can solve my problems.

This simple statement says it all. There is that reaffirmation that Dr. Phil would be happy about "I can solve my problems." There is the assertion of a reality that would make most psychologists pleased "I cannot solve all of my problems." There is the recognition of a time constraint "today" which successful business people will appreciate.

What it means to different people should be thrown out as we think about the simplicity of the statement. Another way of saying it is to say:

Time prevents me from handling everything I need to handle today BUT I can handle everything I have to handle.

Here is yet another way of saying it:

I can manage all of the issues I need to manage. I just cannot do it all today.

Each different way of saying it emphasizes a different part of the adage. Sometimes you need to focus on the time element of the statement. Sometimes you need to focus on the confidence in saying you can handle all of your problems. Sometimes you have to focus on the reality that all of the things you need to do cannot be done in one day.

This adage has served me well at times when I have felt overwhelmed. Problems and the need to solve them can be overwhelming. As a result, the adage creates perspective in allowing me to face only the some of the problems within the time constraint of a single day. In considering that everything I need to do cannot be done today however, I do not fail to appreciate that everything needs to be done at some time. Putting problems off indefinitely is not a solution to those problems.

Those of you familiar with my work are no doubt saying to yourselves, he is not that bright so where did he come up with this wisdom? Give me some credit as it is simple. Like me. But for those of you who cannot grant me that much credit (here comes the subtle transition into another anecdote) I learned this from Owen, the guy who owned three bait shops. Yes, I said bait shops. Here is what he taught me.

Owen had been the owner of three bait shops scattered through the Chain of Lakes that extend down through northern Illinois. Each of his shops contained bait and tackle as well as fishing licenses, fuel for boats, small motors, life jackets, food and things that fisherpeople might need (notice I did not say fishermen because if you cannot be politically correct when talking about bait shops then when can you be). The three shops were located within a radius of about fifteen miles. Owen had three managers, one at each shop. He basically did all the running around between the three shops and he used the one in the middle of the other two as his headquarters.

What set Owen apart from anyone I had ever met in business for themselves was the fact that he was happy. He was not merely content. He was downright happy. He loved the business. He loved the customers. He loved the worms and leaches. He loved the smell of fish. You could say he was as happy as a clam although I have never known what makes clams especially happy. I helped Owen from time to time with trivial matters but for the most part, he really had little use for a lawyer. He never got sued. There seems to be little or no malpractice in the bait shop industry I guess.

"Hey these worms suck. Sorry about that we'll exchange them, try these. Thanks dude." That was about as litigious as it got.

I happened to be fishing one Sunday morning and I decided to visit Owen at his main store. Having gotten off to a late start, I arrived at his bait shop around 7:00 AM. For the first time I could ever recall, when I arrived everything seemed to be in a complete state of turmoil. Owen was not there. The manager of that store had told me that one of the supply trucks for fuel failed to arrive on Friday as scheduled. One of the local worm suppliers: a fourteen year old from down the street who had a shovel, a patch of soil staked off in the woods and a lot of ambition, was sick. He also told me that a group of Owen's regulars was to arrive at about eight o'clock at one of the other stores.

The manager also told me that the power was out at the third store and the manager there was concerned that the refrigerated items would go bad if it did not go back on very soon. When I inquired about Owen's whereabouts in the wake of this chaos, the manager told me that he was out but that he was due back soon.

I almost relished seeing what this type of day would be like for the mild mannered Owen. I felt that the stress of being an attorney was profound compared to the stress free existence of merely running a bait shop. Now I felt that I would see what would happen to Owen in a real crisis.

About fifteen minutes later, Owen arrived. He said hello to me and briefly explained that things had not been going so well. He then went to speak to the manager. In all, he seemed unflappable despite the pandemonium. Not being a complete ass, I decided to offer my assistance. I walked to the office and saw Owen giving the manager some instructions. He looked at me briefly. I offered my help and Owen told me that he appreciated that. He told me he had a job for me.

Then I saw one of the truly great managers I had ever seen perform under incredible pressure without missing a beat. It was inspiring. The amount of control over the situation despite the time constraints made me realize that Owen was indeed a very potent figure in the bait industry and would be in almost any other industry.

Owen instructed the manager to help him take three five gallon gas cans out of Owen's SUV. He explained to the manager that he was to sell no more than five gallons before nine o'clock and another five gallons no earlier than 11:00 AM and then four gallons after that. He was to hold one gallon in case someone had an emergency. If anyone asked for more gas before the allotted time then the manager was to tell them that they were out. He explicitly told him to tell the people that usually they had gas but this week they were out. After that, he told the manager that he was going to the store where the power was out to transport refrigerated items to the store where his regulars were coming. Owen had already phoned the manager there and instructed him to have everything ready to be taken to the other store. He would close the store as a result of the power being out. He then told the manager that I would be able to help with the worm problem.

Owen told me to get into his truck where he handed me a small shovel and proceeded to drive me to a place near the store that had fertile ground for worms. I was to dig up as many as I could and to walk back to the store and give them to the manager. I was told I had one hour for this project and that I would not be respectable unless I returned at least 8 dozen worms..

Meanwhile, Owen had already filled ten five gallon gas can with fuel and was off to meet his regulars. After dropping three off at the main store, he would have eight available for his regulars. Realizing that eight would not be enough, he had me syphon five gallons from my car as well.

In the truck on the way to my worm assignment, I commended him. He shrugged and told me it was nothing. I asked him how much revenue he would lose from the closed store. I will never forget what his answer was. He said it with such clarity of thought and emotion that I could never forget.

He said, "It doesn't matter. I cannot do anything about it so why calculate it? I myself cannot produce electricity therefore I cannot get bogged down in that problem, can I? You see, if you can't do something about it then wondering what it will cost you or how much you could make is wasted thought."

He dropped me off and I went about collecting worms. For the record, I found 114. That was more than respectable by Owen's standards. I was so pleased. I headed back to the store veiled in my triumph. When I told the manager I had 114 worms he gave me a courteous but concerned look. I told him that Owen said that 8 dozen would be respectable in an hour. He snickered at that. When I asked why he laughed he demonstrated some embarrassment and promptly apologized. I told him that I thought I had done well. Then, patronizingly, he said, "oh you did. You should be proud. We appreciate it." I told him to cut the crap. He told me that he did not want to hurt my feelings. I reassured him that he would not. I told him to be brutally honest as to why a mere 114 worms in an hour was even remotely funny. When he was sure he could be honest without me feeling bad, he told me that the high school kid (I told them to call him "worm boy") usually gets about 10 dozen every half hour. He looked at his watch and said, "if Owen said 100 worms by 8:00, then he must have had some pretty low expectations of you." I was so embarrassed that I asked for my shovel back and ran back to my post to dig up some more worms. I obtained about another 63 before I could find absolutely no more. I have no idea how that kid gets 120 in a half hour. I wanted to meet "wormboy" though.

Shortly after I returned, Owen was just coming back. He had scrounged another ten gallons of gas and had some extra food and bait from the shop he closed for the day. He asked me how things went with the worms. I told him that I had collected almost 200 before 8:00. He told me that the kid had once brought back about that much in twenty minutes. Forget meeting him, I wanted to kill "wormboy." That little subterranean psychopath should meet a girl or get a hobby or something. It has to be steroids.

Owen quickly went about his business after that. He remained calm as ever as the manager reported that they were low on fuel and, unfortunately, worms. They discussed the situation. His regular customers were due to arrive at the other store in about twenty minutes. They would need about fifteen gallons of gas and plenty of bait, food and drinks. He raided what he could from this store and readied to return to the other store before his regulars arrived. In watching the stress not even causing him to break a sweat, I asked him if he was okay.

He assured me that he was. I told him that anyone else would have a heart attack working as fast and as hard as he was. I asked him how he did it. That is when he said it to me. He stated it not as succinctly as I would eventually make it but he stated it clearly.

He said, "Look , I have a great many problems and I can handle all of them. Now all I have to do is prioritize them and take care of them in order. I might not get to all of them today but I can handle all of them."

The next day he called me to thank me again for the help. I realized that I should be thanking him. He had taught me one of the best secrets I had learned about time and stress management. I did not want to give in however. I did not thank him. Instead, I sent him a bill for my hourly rate of $195.00 for digging up the worms. I would like to see "wormboy" do that.

Ultimately, what Owen taught me was what I had said before. "I can handle all of my problems I just cannot handle all of them today." Or "I cannot solve all of my problems today but, I can solve my problems." Either way, it is a descent tool for handling time and stress management.

As Owen understood, it all comes down to handling what you can. He had the ability to think on his feet. He also did not get bogged down in problems he could not solve such as the store without electricity. He prioritized handling his regular customers. He used resources such as me to address the worm problem.

Now the problems you may face one day may be much more significant than those in Owen's bait shop but the principles remain the same. So long as you know that you can handle all the problems that you have and so long as you can realistically deal with your time constraints, you too can manage your business when the sky is falling. Just tell yourself that you can handle all of your problems but that you cannot handle all of them today.

In the end, Owen addressed a series of problems and by keeping cool, recognizing his limitations and by believing in himself, he prevented letting his many problems become a calamity.

CHAPTER 4
Complaining about the Weather:
Coping

There is an old adage, as far as I can tell it has never been more than an adage. It goes like this:

"There is no sense in complaining about the weather."

The statement is simple and true and it addresses the issues that we face when trying to cope with things in operating our businesses. The concept is simple enough. All it means is that you should not complain about things that you cannot control. Think about it. What sense does it make to complain about the weather? You cannot do anything that is going to affect it. Now I know that there are hyper critical (as opposed to regular) environmentalists who will differ on this point by saying "well if we cut down on the use of fluorocarbons we would save the ozone and potentially stop certain atmospheric changes that could ultimately change the weather." This type of logic misses the point by so much that I cannot explain it to them. Thanks for buying my book hyper critical environmentalists, I am sorry that it made no sense to you.

Now that we have sufficiently offended hyper critical environmentalists, the point is that you cannot do anything about the weather TODAY. So if you cannot do anything to affect the weather (today) why spend time, effort and emotion complaining about it.

Face it, complaining takes effort. So why do some people complain? Some feel satisfaction in letting others know that they are being challenged by forces beyond them. Some complain for the mere satisfaction of releasing frustration over many things and different issues and focusing it on a single issue. For them, they may complain about the weather because they cannot complain about other things in their lives. Complaining about the other things might open the door to more problems or might reflect badly on them so they keep their opinions about these things to themselves and they complain about the things they can complaint about.

For example, a husband might come home and trip on a toy left on the floor of the living room. His wife had a half day at work and has been home for five hours already. She could have picked up the toy but did not. But he will not complain about his wife because their anniversary is the next day and he realizes that complaining about the untidy house may cost him if he has any romantic plans for the following day. Now realize that he hurt himself when he tripped and afterwards wanted to kick the toy through an open window but, he cannot because the toy he stops himself from kicking belongs to his kid who was home from school with a temperature and a headache. He sees no sense in starting a crying fit by the kid or himself. So the man sees the dog loudly sipping water out of his water dish and he promptly complains, "That God blessed dog is so freaking loud I am sick of it. He can't even sip water without being annoying! I have had enough of that crappy canine! He's driving me nuts! You pain in the ass dog!" Safe in realizing that the dog cannot fight back and will not really be bothered by the complaint nor will it cry uncontrollably, the husband can complain about the dog to cope with the things that are really frustrating him.

Some people complain as an opening to arguing or debating a point. It goes like this: "You know, this mayor sucks. Our police force is in a shambles, there is garbage in the streets. Our schools are terrible and our taxes are too high!" So you think to yourself, wow this guy really has a lot of complaints. Then, you hear him say, "If I were mayor . . . . . . vote for me."

The point here is to analyze and assess why certain people complain about certain things. Then, you also need to realize and assess why you complain about certain things. Are you complaining about the real issues bothering you or are you frustrated about something else that you are not willing to admit? Are you complaining so as to persuade people to do something? Then focus on your business. Am I complaining about the business because I no longer like the business? Is the business making me so unhappy or even so miserable that I need to complain about it?

In assessing whether the business is making you complain let me put your fears to rest. The business is causing you to complain. It is the business's fault. Your business makes you unhappy and often times miserable. Now does that feel better? The business has been responsible for making you complain. You have the answer.   The question now becomes, do I want to do something about it or do I just want to quit? If you want to do something about it, keep reading. If you want to quit, skip to Chapter 35 "Should I stay or Should I Go."

Good for you, if you are still with me. So if you do not want to quit and you want to do something about the complaints, you have to do some investigating. You need to find the cause of your frustration. That is all it is by the way. It is just frustration that leads to complaints. You know about handling frustration because you overcame frustration long enough to start your own business. Now by assessing what is making you frustrated and determining what to do about it, if anything, you can either overcome the frustration or you can learn to avoid useless complaining.

In your business, think about the things you complain about. Maybe you have a vendor whose service is terrible. Do you complain about it? If this vendor is the cheapest and you are on a budget then can you complain? What if this vendor is the only one in town and it would cut you off without thinking about it if you did complain. This example is an important part of your assessment. Can you complain about this situation? If you are stuck in this situation, does it do you any good to complain? If you can complain, what would be the consequence of it?

You need to face it. There are certain things in business that you cannot do anything about so it does no good to complain about it. It is like complaining about the weather. There is nothing good that can come from complaining about the weather. But, for all its worthlessness, we still feel the need to complain even if we cannot change the situation.

Maybe, we have a psychological need to complain. We hear the phrase bandied about all the time "oh he was just venting." What a euphemism that is: "Venting." To call complaining merely "venting" is bad for two reason. First, it reinforces the idea that people need to "vent" or, in essence, they need to complain. That term makes it sound as though it is something someone has to do like you would a barbecue pit. "You need to vent it and let a little steam out." Reinforcing the need to complain gives it some sort of psychological value but does not make it profitable however. The second reason that the phrase "venting" is bad is that it demonstrates a gender bias in the business world today that has yet to be fully overcome. If a woman is complaining it is referred to as "ragging" or "bitching." But if a guy is complaining people say, "oh he's just venting." Nevertheless, whether you call it "venting," "ragging," "bitching," or just plain old complaining, all of us at one time or another feel the need to do it. Because the need is so deeply rooted in our psyche, I guess that there is no use in complaining about the fact that we need to complain.

But, if we need to complain, then is there any way to generate some value out of what we complain about? If not, then it is imperative that we strive to make certain that our senseless complaining is policed to assure that it does not hurt the business too badly.

It would be hard to make an argument that complaining about the things we cannot change could be profitable. It belies common sense to think that any waste of time such as complaining could make your business more profitable or likely to achieve any of its goals. Perhaps, complaining is a stall tactic for some to allow them time to think. In other cases, it might be used by the business operator to push others away at times when he or she needs to be alone to think. This does not make it profitable but it does give it some value. Sometimes, complaining provides solidarity among people who all have the same complaint. "You said it! This weather sucks!" There might be some perceived value in that but still, it would be hard to quantify or qualify its value.

If we proceed on the theory that complaining serves no profitable purpose but that it will happen anyway, then, as we said, we need to police it effectively. In assessing useless complaining, determine what people in the business complain about and to whom. Nothing undermines a business more than one person complaining to another about someone else. It undermines confidences amongst staff members. It creates disunity and an "us and them" atmospheres. If you are the boss, never complain about one employee to another employee. These alliances seldom work on "Survivor" and they do not work in business. Finally, when complaining goes unchecked it creates an atmosphere of unsatisfied and disgusted people who are not pleasant to be around. If you care about how much people like being around you, monitor how much you complain during a given day. if you can say one positive thing for every complaint you make, then people will see you as fair minded and balanced. People are drawn to balanced people.

To make things a little more complicated, think about what really constitutes "complaining." Distinguish it from "constructive criticism." Make sure that it does not become merely criticizing. People can accept complaints but, they do not like having constant complaints about their job performance. It becomes belittling. You must also make sure that criticism does not get dressed up in a useless complaint. "I know that you did not have enough time to finish this project because of other things that came up, but you really are slow when it comes to doing these things that I ask you to do." This comment is useless as both a complaint and a criticism. You tell the person that you are aware of a legitimate reason why they could not finish a task and then you complain about other tasks that they have performed that have nothing to do with what you are complaining about. What could possibly be gained from such a statement? An upset or pissed off employee: that is what. We all know how valuable those are.

So, if you will be allowing useless complaining to exist, you need to watch it carefully. Do not let it get out of hand and do not let it become an epidemic. If you complain too much, your staff will feel that it is okay. Your ability to control it will force them to do the same. If you keep it to a minimum, then if people in your organization complain too much, you can lead the rest of the staff in ostracizing the complainers and eliminating the behavior. You can set the tone that needlessly complaining is not acceptable and make the people who complain about useless things look foolish and immature. The trick, is to ostracize the complainers without complaining about them.

When should you complain.

Are there times when you have a right to legitimately complain? The answer depends on your ability to distinguish between complaining when you can do something about the cause of the frustration and when you cannot. For example, you cannot complain about your nearest competitor winning the lottery because like the weather, you cannot do anything about it. If you lack the capacity to control the outcome of some situation, then complaining about it makes no sense. However, if you can control future events in a given situation, then complaining may have some benefit.

If your sales force is putting in less than 100%, you can complain about that to them in the hope of pushing them to increase sales. In this situation, the complaining has to be properly focused on the future rather than the past. It is useless to say, "these past sales figures are horrible, this whole company is going down hill." The focus here is on the past and the complaint makes the future look bleak. Worse yet, the way that the complaint is structured, it makes it look as though the bleak future is already accepted and expected. The funny thing about failure is that if you expect it, you will seldom be surprised.

A more appropriate way to complain in that situation is to focus on a better future. You could say, "the past sales figures are horrible, we have to do better." This complaint is more useful. It has a positive imperative for the future. There is a compulsion here to force a better result in the future despite a past that is worth complaining about. In this way, you demonstrate that your complaint is not an end in itself. Your complaint is a prelude to identifying a bad situation and making the future better.

The complaint identifies a problem that needs a solution. You need to recognize that this is the only value of a complaint. Complaints that identify problems that have no solution have no value. If you can make this distinction, then you can determine when it is appropriate to complain.

Take four letters out of the word complain and you have "Camp" No, "Coma" NO TRY "Plan."

If you are going to take the time to complain then you should also make the time to offer a plan to do something about it. People who complain and do nothing about it lack motivation. We see them all the time. They are typically the cynical people who have a nasty remark about everything. They have nothing positive to say about anything and they never offer any hope that things will get better. They are malcontents. They never offer any suggestion as to how to fix a problem they only point out the problem. The reason why they are this way is simple. To offer a proposal or a possible solution involves risk. Malcontents do not wish to risk offering a plan to change things because the plan might not be successful. There is a risk that they will be wrong. They would rather accentuate the negative and appear pessimistic than risk offering a solution that might work. They could not endure the humility, not humiliation necessarily, that results from being wrong.

You are in business for yourself. You are not one of these people. You can risk being wrong in trying to change a bad situation that is worth complaining about. Offering a solution that does not work is better than merely complaining without offering any solution. And if a problem has no solution, then it is not worth complaining about anyway. But if a solution can be tried, then the complaint is not useless.

In Chicago, we have a saying, "the Cubs suck." I guess that 98 years without winning a World Series will make you say that. The complaint, as stated however, is useless. It might be better to say, "the Cubs have been really bad but, if they reorganize the talent, manage game situations better, focus on consistently good pitching as opposed to occasional great pitching, then maybe the Cubs can turn things around." (Note to the Chicago Tribune, as I write this you are currently considering three or four candidates for a new manager. This is not an attempt on my part to make it five. Thanks anyway but I am busy.).

The only point here is that if you can identify a problem by way of complaining, and you can put together a plan to attack the problem, then the complaint is not such a bad thing. It is not necessarily a waste of time. So long as it results in you taking some affirmative steps to change the situation or address the problem, then the complaint might have some merit.

The opposite of those people who cynically complain without risking offering a solution are the overly optimistic souls who merely "hope" that things will get better. We have all seen them. Their complaints are so delightfully naive that they make us sick. "Our team did poorly this year and failed to make the post season but we will be better next year." These people are not offering a solution. They are offering blind hope that things will be better not a plan for making things better. These people always throw around the platitude, "it will be okay, things will work out." You need to be wiser than that. You need to recognize that if things are not going well and you do nothing to change them, you should have no expectation that they will get better or "work out." Moreover, you do not merely need to hope that things get better you need to perform some act that will makes things better. That act requires planning. If things are not what you want them to be then you need to take affirmative steps to change them. You cannot merely hope that the situation will change.

Unless, of course, it is a situation that you cannot control. For example, "the weather sucked last night but I hope that it is better today."

The best analogy of all of what we have covered can be seen in the common practice in many businesses known as the "suggestion box." We have all seen them. It is the old box on the wall that allows employees to anonymously provide an opinion on some topic to make the company better. As we open our box we see all types of complaints, problems and possible solutions. Our first note says: "The day starts too early." That is all of it. We all know the type of person who writes that. They need their sleep so they complain about how early the day starts. There are no specifics. The day actually starts at midnight. There is nothing you can do about that. Otherwise, if they are talking about the work day, well that is pretty much dictated by the normal course of business and you can do little to change that. Therefore, this note is a complaint about a problem that has no solution. Wad it up and send it to the waste paper basket. It is a useless complaint by a cynical employee who is sleep deprived.

The next note says: "too many people are taking advantage of sick days." This is also a complaint. It has no solution on it and seems to be from one of our cynical friends. But it is different in that it identifies a problem that might have a solution. Although the writer offers no solution, the complaint is worth some consideration. You write it down and wad up the note and send it to join the rambling of the sleep deprived guy.

Our next note says: "The lines in the parking lot have faded and the lot is becoming too full, we need to repaint the lines and fix some of the potholes." I like this employee. He or she has a complaint that identifies a problem and offers a solution. Maybe you should fix the potholes as that might create more useable parking spaces. Maybe you should re-stripe the lot and make the individual spots slightly more narrow to allow for more cars. This might or might not be a good idea but it is an idea. Like anything else, it might be worth a try.

Another note says, "The vending machines in the cafeteria are always running out of Butterfingers, I hope that we could get some more." This is a complaint that points out a problem. As a Butterfingers fan, I would say that it is a serious problem. The note offers nothing more than a wish that the problem gets solved however. Throw the note away and call the vending machine supplier to help this guy out.

The last note says, "Tom in accounting lost his dog on a camping trip, we hope that he's okay." This is a nice note. We are either hoping that Tom or his dog are okay. Personally, I hope that both are okay. We cannot do anything about this but it is nice to hope that the dog and his master will be reunited soon. Toss the note and say a prayer.

So, let me summarize my points regarding complaining. If you are going to complain about a problem that has no solution, then the complaining is useless. If you are going to complain about a problem that might have a solution but you are not offering a solution then you are useless and the complaint might have some value. If you are going to complain about a problem that has a solution and you are merely going to hope that the problem gets solved than you are useless and the complaint has some value. And finally, the only time it is appropriate to merely hope that things get better and not take some action pursuant to a plan to make things better is when you are hoping that a situation that causes a complaint that you cannot do anything about gets better. "The weather sucked today and I hope that it is better tomorrow."

CHAPTER 5
Things You do not Fret Over but that You Should

Since we have talked about how to handle the little problems that often times cause stress, we turn our attention to the big problems that should cause stress but for many entrepreneurs never do. There are things that you should be worried about. More importantly, there are things that should be worthy of your stress. These things are not the everyday responsibilities such as payroll and taxes. Those things should be important and necessarily must be done. Because they must be done, they really should not be stressful. They do not require a great amount of deliberation they simply must be done. Productivity, efficiency, thrift and decision-making are things that can be stressful as you operate your business but they can be swallowed up by the big things in your business that you should feel stress over. Sadly, few business owners stress the truly important things and become weighted down in the other matters. Concentration on the individual trees tends to obscure the forest for these people.

So what should you be stressing over? You need to ask yourself some questions. Does your business have a message? Does it have a personality? Does your business have a purpose? Existentialists refer to this as a raison d'etre. It means a reason for being. You should feel stress over the more cosmic place your business serves in the universe. You need to feel stress over that aspect of your business that exists beyond your simple everyday problems and consider whether there is a reason for your business to exist. If you cannot think of the reason, that should be causing you stress.

Why should these things cause you stress? Well, in the first place, if you cannot identify the reason for your business existing then why are you running it in the first place. Beyond the platitudes of merely operating the business for money, you need a particular reason for operating your particular business.

Sometimes the best way to identify your business's reason for being is to identify the message that it sends to the general public. If you operate a service business, does your business send out a message that you have years of experience? Or, does your business's message say that your business never fails its customers? Or, does your message say: you care about your customers? Does your message say: we are the cheapest or we are the best or we are for people with discriminating taste or we are efficient, or we are friendly?   You need to know what message your business is sending out.

You need to stress over whether your business sends out the wrong messages such as: we are too busy to really help you, or we are cheap and impolite; or only sometimes do we get it right; or you might do better with our competitor. In these situations, as these messages go out to the public, your business's reason for being is either to merely exist as a poor alternative to your competition or to exist merely to do the least necessary for its customers. Provided that these are not the messages you want to send, you have to ask yourself another question. Is the true or intended message and personality of my business being conveyed?

This brings us to the only thing in business that should constantly be on your mind and should always be the one thing that should cause you stress. You need to constantly question whether your business's reason for existing and the message it intends to send out is consistent with the public's perception of the business. All three aspect need to be consistent. You should not have a reason for existing that differs from the message being sent out because that will result in an inconsistency as to what the public perceives of the business.

Essentially, if you set a specific reason for your business to exist, your success in the business is measured by how closely the public perceives that reason. The public's perception comes from the message that the business sends. Therefore, your ability to have the business fulfill its reason for existing and then causing the public to view the business in that way is what should be your focus. Because this requires dynamic and complex thinking on your part, it should be stressful.

To say that it is stressful does not mean all the worst of what that term conveys however. To say that you should stress, or simply worry about whether the business's stated purpose and its message are consistent with the public's image of the business does not imply that it should keep you up at night. To say that this is worthy of your worry and potentially worthy of your stress is to say that perpetually failing to maintain the consistency of the business's purpose, message and public perception is the type of thing that should keep you up at night. For most entrepreneurs, it is the only thing that should keep them up at night.

Why is it so important? There are many reasons but the simplest and best reason for maintaining the business's purpose, message and public perception is that there is no other way to evaluate the success of the business. Without thinking about those things, you are not working towards you ultimate goal. What is worse is that for so many entrepreneurs, this does not cause them stress. It really never enters their mind. Too many entrepreneurs never really think about what the business stands for and what the public perceives about the business. The dangers of this should be evident.

Thinking about the business's purpose, message and public image can be anywhere from merely abstract to beyond cosmic. These are heavy thoughts. It takes a great deal of brain muscle to hold and carry them. That may be why they are stressful. Because you need to think about these things every day and because you need to factor them into every major decision, it should be a focal point for how you evaluate the business.

Here is an example. I opened my law practice to be a one stop shop for the needs of small business owners to have a single attorney handle everything from formation to transactions to litigation to winding up the organization. If a client came to me for a closing on the purchase of a building and was happy with my services but then went to another attorney to defend it in a lawsuit, then my purpose and message were lost on that client. I have to ask myself, how come that client did not get the message from me that I could handle the litigation for them. How come that client did not see my firm as a "one stop" shop dedicated to all types of business issues including more than handling a real estate transaction? In this instance, because my message was not being conveyed, I lost the opportunity to do more business with the client. That causes me stress as I wonder why I did not get the message out that I could handle this other matter for the client.

The most important thing to take from that experience is the understanding and the determination to make sure that I convey to the next client that I can handle all types of matters for them. I need for them to perceive that my firm is the go to guy for all of their needs regarding their business. So long as I worry about that and think about it, I should not necessarily feel all the wrong types of stress over it.

How does one develop a business purpose, message and public perception? That should not be stressful. These things develop in many different ways. Perhaps it is one of the most interesting things in business that someone opens a business with one stated purpose and over time, another one develops.

That can happen. Sometimes the business has a mind of its own for reasons beyond its owner's control. As a result, the business might develop a purpose, message and image of its own. This is not something to worry about SO LONG AS you know what the purpose, message and image are. Of course, if the purpose, message and image are not consistent or not appropriate or simply could result in loss of profits or wasted efforts, then you need to change them.

Nevertheless, many businesses develop a purpose, message and image of their own. Many owners will resent that they lose control over the purpose, message and image. As an owner, you need to think of the business as separate from yourself. As a result, you may control the business, but like one of your children, it is separate from you. In this way, entrepreneurs need to recognize that they are merely an ingredient in the development of the purpose, message and image of their businesses. If there are several owners or entrepreneurs involved, then each becomes an ingredient in those things. If there are key employees, then they too become an ingredient. How many times have you seen a business whose customers relate to one of the salesmen as if he owned the place. His personality may be part of the message sent by the business. If you hired him because his personality is consistent with the purpose you had in mind, then he too becomes and ingredient in what becomes the business's message and image.

A keen business owner needs to also consider that the purpose, message and image will change over time. Sometimes this will occur naturally usually in response to changing market conditions. Sometimes, it will be planned as when new employees, owners or shareholders become involved in the business. We have all seen this. The father and mother give the business to a son or daughter who have worked it and the business changes. Sometimes those changes are good and frequently they are bad. But because there is some new ingredient in what makes up the business, the business now sends out a new message and develops a new image.

As the business's purpose, message and image change over time, that should also cause you stress as you need to constantly watch and monitor all three. For all the other things in business to worry about, these three things are the most overlooked and yet may very well be the most important.

CHAPTER 6
Maybe MacDonald's said it best: "You Deserve a Break Today"

Once you have been working your own business for a while, sometimes stress develops from the tedium and routine. The phrase "daily grind" becomes all too appropriate as an adequate description of this syndrome. This type of stress is not the result of any one occurrence but is instead the culmination of accumulating stressful events. These events are well within your capacity to handle on a one by one basis. But, over time, as you handle one after another after another after another, you become worn down. Your immunity to the little tensions becomes compromised simply because you have endured one after another in succession.

The danger to this type of stress is that it sneaks up on you. You hardly notice it because it develops over time. It is increasingly hard to predict how it will hit you or when it will get to the point where it will cause your anxiety to boil over. Much like a volcano, you can never be sure when the aggregate of all these little annoyances, obstacles and pressure will force you to blow.

There are two things that must be done in order to prevent this type of stress from making you prematurely grey. First, you need to monitor your stress levels and then you need to diffuse the stress you feel. It might seem simple, and I wish that it could be, but there is a trick to it.

In monitoring your stress, you need to watch for signs. Are you becoming irritable at the small stuff? Are you finding it hard to concentrate? Wait, stop right there. I know that you are in business for yourself and everything makes you irritable and it is always hard to concentrate. In order to monitor it, however, you need to assess whether you are more irritable than normal and whether you are having a harder time concentrating than you typically do. You need to take a step back and ask yourself, "am I on edge?"

One of the best ways to know if you are on edge is to look at your motivation levels. Do you feel that you want to give it your all to accomplish your goals or are you merely going through the motions? As new business opportunities present themselves are you happy and eager to get started or are you merely dreading more work? When you arrive in the morning, do you feel that you are looking forward to all that you can get done that day or are you just waiting for the end of the day? Quite simply, are you motivated to lead the business or are you letting it carry you?

Let me start by saying that it is okay to feel this way. That is fine. The business does owe you. The problem is that you cannot allow these feelings to persist. The business needs you to lead it and to be motivated to make it grow and prosper. Much like a parent to a child, the kids need mom or dad to show them the way and be there for them and to take care of things. But, like any parent will tell you at some point it becomes difficult, if not impossible, to always do everything for your kids. At that point, you need a break.

So, once you have monitored your stress levels and have recognized that your motivation is falling off then you need to take a break. It is odd that we call it a "break." It happens at a "breaking point" in most cases. But, referring to it as a "break" seems to fit the concept of stopping something. You need to be away from the everyday stress caused by the business. You need to remove yourself from the tension of the business. You need to get out of the rut you feel you are in because of the business. You need a break from the business.

Feeling guilty? You might. Any parent might feel terrible about wanting to be away from the kids for a while. It is natural. You feel that you are not a good parent or entrepreneur for not wanting to be with your kids or your business for a period of time. What happened to that seemingly endless infatuation you once had for your kids or your business? You used to think that they were fascinating and that you could never want to be away. How do you get that feeling back?

Someone once said, "Absence makes the heart grow fonder." I once said, "Abstinence makes the erection harder." Vulgar as it is, it is true. Taking time away from anything can reinvigorate your feelings towards it. It can allow you to regain perspective and find your appreciation for it all over again. Removing yourself for a time from anyone or anything that you deal with day in and day out can benefit your relationship with that person or thing.

Mentally, because entrepreneurs are driven as they are, and because they are wired the way they are, they need distractions in order to regain an

43

appreciation for their business venture. That distraction can usually only be effective when it completely removes the person from his or her business. The most valuable distractions to an entrepreneur are those that cause you to completely "reset." Like any device with a reset button, you need to be turned off for a moment and reset. You need to start fresh sometimes. A reset can sometimes cause the device to work properly or even more efficiently after it has encountered problems.

Basically, what this means is that you need a distraction that is sufficiently powerful enough to make you forget about the business for a while. You need something that can take your mind to a completely different place away from anything even related to the business.

What should you do? Watch a good movie. Read a mystery or thriller novel. (Note: try "The Pardoner's Tale" "The Winter" or "Unconnected" by Scott Annes. Any of these may be very good reads.). Watch or attend a sporting event. Watch some coach deal with his or her problems on the field with his or her players and forget about your own for a while. Engage in a sporting event. Golf makes me forget about work, my kids, my wife, my swing . . . You might even try a vacation.

Whatever you do, take a break that takes you away. Even if you cannot get away physically, take a break that gets you away mentally. Let me rephrase and emphasize that point. You do not need to physically get away. But, you must get away mentally.

If you are going to take a break, take a break without guilt. Make sure that whatever you plan your distraction to be you commit to it as a distraction and let it serve its purpose. Guilt has no purpose in taking a break. If you accept the fact that taking a break is necessary and valuable to your operation of the business, then there should be no reason to feel guilty. The reason why you should eliminate the guilt is that sometimes you might be proud of the fact that you never take breaks. Maybe you disdain people who need them. If the pressure and stress of operating a business does not cause you to need a break then good for you. But, do not be a martyr about not taking breaks. If you need one, take one and do not feel guilty about it. Do not judge yourself for needing a break and do not berate yourself for succumbing to the pressure of running your own business. The only thing you owe to the business is doing whatever is necessary to make it successful. Because most people can use a break now and then in order to more effectively run the business, you owe it to the business to freshen up your enthusiasm for the business now and then. Taking a break accomplishes this.

PART II
Entrepreneurial Attitude

Chapter 7
Do I Have any Clue in the world what the hell I'm doing?

Well do you?   If you are in business for yourself and you have been for any length of time you might ask this question of yourself from time to time. It is a fair question. It demonstrates that, on occasion, you question yourself and possibly your ability. If you do so on a limited basis so as to create perspective, then by all means question yourself from time to time. If you obsess over whether you know what you are doing, well . . . .

Mothers tell their children "believe in yourself."   That was fine when you were a kid but if you have to consciously think about believing in yourself then you have got bigger problems.   Believing in yourself is not a brain exercise. You cannot simply say: "Okay, today I'm going to believe in myself. I know what my situation is and I know I can tell myself that I can handle it. I'm the man! No really, I'm the mannnnnnn! I can fist pump like Tiger Woods, I'm the greatest. Yeah, I'm the best baby!"

Say all of that to yourself in the mirror and you will recognize how ridiculous it is to have to think about believing in yourself. Look, you do not have time to watch Dr. Phil. His show is on during the day and you should be working at that time anyway. You are running a business for God's sake. You do not need talk show cheerleaders to tell you to empower yourself. That stuff is for people who do not yet have the gumption to do what you have already done. The people who need that stuff are people who are trying to find themselves. They lack the motivation to actually find themselves because they fear what they will find. So they tell themselves that they are looking but they know not to look anywhere that they can possibly, even by mistake, find themselves.

46

You are not like that. You have accomplished something already with your life. You are in business. You have committed to something in your life. You do not have to find yourself. You do not have the time. Your time is too precious and valuable to stop and consciously think about believing in yourself because you can do it automatically.

Unlike the poor fools sitting home on their couches, you are not wondering whether you have the ability to perform a task, achieve a goal, solve a problem, or conquer an insurmountable obligation. Those people are home because they are focusing on whether they possess the ability to face those things. You are an entrepreneur. You do not have the time to wonder whether you have the ability to do those things. You are too busy focusing on doing those things. While they are wondering if they can handle those things, you are wondering how you will tackle those things. Your focus is completely different.

The old saying about getting your head out of your ass clarifies this distinction. While the poor fools at home are looking into themselves, probably through their own ass, you are an entrepreneur looking outside of yourself. You do not have to reassure yourself that you can handle your problems because you have got problems to handle. You are smart enough to realize that wondering whether you can handle a problem does not solve the problem. I will go even farther. Convincing yourself that you can handle your problem does not solve the problem. Try this. Solve the problem and then you will know that you can solve the problem.

But what about those days when you wonder if you are right? What about those days when you have to think about if what you are doing is the right course of action in any given situation or in every situation? What about those times when you question yourself?

Actually, within certain limits, it is okay to look at what you are doing from time to time. An occasional personal assessment can be beneficial. It can get you to refocus. It can reestablish humility. It can also provide insight into yourself. That too can be beneficial. Perhaps, most importantly, it allows for you to perform one of the best business maneuvers that are often overlooked but more often necessary. That maneuver is called "course correction."

The fateful Apollo 13 astronauts had been on a course to return to the Earth after having circumnavigated the moon. At some point on that

47

return, they had drifted off course. Although they were still headed toward the Earth, they needed to perform a "course correction" in order to assure that they would return at precisely the right trajectory in order to avoid skidding off the Earth's atmosphere and thereby missing the chance to return safely. They had a destination and they were aiming toward it but they needed to make an adjustment in order to make certain that they hit the destination just right.

Course correction is a maneuver that is defined as the small to moderate change in direction or path to assist in arriving at one's destination. Recognizing that it might be a change in direction OR path is critical. Changing direction implies that you were headed the wrong way. Changing your path means that you have found another way to get to the destination without necessarily changing direction. Performing a course correction does not mean that you are changing your destination. It means that your destination or your goal remains the same but the manner in which you get there or achieve your goal can change.

This is the value of questioning yourself. If you are focused on your goal and your goal does not change, then you can think about different ways of achieving the goal. In questioning whether you are right or wrong about anything, you need to look at what you question. Are you questioning your goal or the ultimate destination or are you questioning how you are going to get there?

People who question their goals are the ones who wonder what the hell they are doing. People who know their ultimate goal but question how they are going about achieving it are usually just in business for themselves. If you are doing the soul searching to wonder what you ultimately are looking to accomplish or what your goals are, then you have a serious problem. All of your energy is wasted because you are pushing yourself forward but you are not getting to where you want to be necessarily. You might get lucky and get to a place you like to be. Or, you might burn a great deal of energy to get to a place that is far from where you want to be.

The other problem with not knowing your goals is that you cannot assess your progress. When you have a specific destination you can tell how far you are from it during the trip. But, if you have no destination, how do you know if you are closer or farther from where you want to get to? People who are not in business for themselves can ask that question. They can ponder what the ultimate goal for them will be. They can wonder what the hell they are doing.

However, if you are in business for yourself, chances are, whether you consciously think about them or not, you know your ultimate goals. Chances are, you have some idea how to achieve those goals. And, chances are, from time to time, you have changed the way you have gone about trying to arrive at achieving those goals. You have corrected your course.

So if you get passed the question of wondering what you are doing then the only question left to ask yourself is, am I doing what I need to do in order to achieve my goals? If you have asked yourself that question then you are entitled to a hearty CONGRATULATIONS! That is an entrepreneurial question. That one is always okay to ask. It implies so many good things about you. It implies that you know what your goals are. It implies that you are actively assessing your progress in achieving those goals. It implies that you want to pursue a path that gets you to your ultimate destination and that you are willing to consider an occasional course correction to make sure you get there. Nothing about this question implies that you are wandering aimlessly or that you have any intention of wasting your time or effort.

It does not imply lack of confidence on your part either. Just because you might be questioning your route does not mean that you are questioning your destination. You desire is to get to your destination. Determining the best route is a good thing. It means that you are trying to find an efficient and expeditious way of getting there. As you achieve goals, you will learn better and easier routes. You will constantly assess progress and the efficiency of various routes and you will learn that the best question to ask is, what can I do to get where I want to go faster, easier, safer, or simply better. So long as the question "what am I doing" never becomes a derivative of "where am I going?" you will be just fine.

CHAPTER 8
How am I different From Them?

Here you are. You are in business for yourself. You run the show. You have responsibilities, deadlines, timetables, schedules etc. It is up to you. You do have the bonus of being the boss. People listen to you (sometimes). But, there is one nagging question. As you interact with people who are not in business for themselves, you have to ask yourself, "How am I different from them?"

As you think about it, you realize that you are different in a lot of ways. We could talk about how you have a different attitude or how you have different goals for yourself. We could talk about how you are focused on different things and how you face different decisions than they do. We could talk about a great many differences but we need only consider one. By being in business for yourself you have a different perspective than people not in business for themselves. In order to stay in business, you must maintain this different perspective. It will control all that you do.

So what is this "different" perspective? The "different" perspective is found in several components. The first of which is the recognition of your own self-reliance. Unlike people not in business for themselves, you have to see things in terms of your own self-reliance. Whereas your friends who work for other people safely can count on their employer for a paycheck at the end of the week, you have to count on yourself to produce that paycheck. You have only yourself to blame if you do not have that paycheck. Also, if that paycheck is way more than it usually is then you have yourself to thank.

Another major component of the entrepreneur's perspective is an appreciation for the need to be productive or risk losing or not having money. People who are employed by others face significantly less risk than you. They enjoy the safety of a steady paycheck. Absent special circumstances for particular types of employees, there is very little risk of not getting paid for your work. They are dependent upon the employer for their money. You on the other hand are risking not having any money. If you do not work or you do not accomplish anything of value or if you simply fail to collect, you end up without any money to show for the work you have done.

Think about what this does to your perspective. When you were an employee you only had to be as productive as the minimum your employer would tolerate without firing you. Depending on the employer, that could be a pretty low standard. Some employees could be complete slackers who get paid more than they are worth and they know it. But an entrepreneur does not have the luxury of merely achieving this lower standard. Entrepreneurs need to maximize individual productivity in order to receive a paycheck. No one is handing anything to them. Usually.

Why usually? Well there are entrepreneurs who get very lucky and have one significant customer or client. (oh, I don't know, let's make up the name of a customer, we will call it the City of Chicago). The customer, Chicago, hands certain entrepreneurs as much business as their companies can handle. Moreover, that customer might not even require the entrepreneurs to do anything in order to keep the business. For example, for our imaginary customer, Chicago, there might even be times when entrepreneurs get paid not to do any work except maybe on Election Day. There is a difference to these types of entrepreneurs though. They are not self employed in the truest sense of the word. They are wholly owned by their major customers. In that way, they are merely employees of their major customers. And, chances are, if they are merely employees of their major customer, they work under the impression that all they need to do is the minimum necessary in order to keep the customer and not get fired. (By the way, if our imaginary customer, the City of Chicago, wanted to make my little business lucky, my number is in the phonebook).

But, suppose you are not so lucky as to have one super customer. You need to work to make money. If you fail, no money. That causes you to have a significantly different thinking process than people who are merely employees. As a component of you entrepreneurial perspective, this might cause you to weigh decisions more closely. You have a smaller margin for error than people who do not need to worry about their paycheck. You might need to be more cautious than some people and you might have to sweat risks more than mere employees.. You will have more sleepless nights than employees. You are playing for bigger stakes than they are. There are more dire consequences to the decisions you have to make.

Yet another component of entrepreneurial perspective is the amount of time you are working. You are always working as an entrepreneur. Employees work until 5:00 PM. You have to always seek opportunity to grow the business. Employees do not care. Their time off of work is their own. You carry business cards and you take every opportunity to give them out. Employees do not necessarily care about generating more business for the company. In fact, they may want to do less business.

Another component of entrepreneurial perspective that has to do with time is that you wish to make the most of time while employees merely want to make it pass. Time is more important to entrepreneurs than to mere employees. You see time as money. They see time as dragging. Their weekends are too short for the time they had off. Yours are too short for what you could have accomplished.

And still another component of entrepreneurial perspective is the ability to link performance to wealth. If you perform, you gain wealth. If you are successful in having people buy from you, then you acquire wealth. You operate your entire business on a commission basis if you think about it. You might have a regular salary or draw but in the end anything the business makes is based on your level of success in selling what you have to sell. I see independent salespeople who work exclusively for commissions as hybrids of entrepreneurs and standard employees. They might have a base and some benefits, but, their personal wealth and success is based on their own achievement. If they make a sale, they make money. If not, well . . . . for your purposes, you need to recognize that your personal level of performance in selling forms the basis for the success of your business.

When we assess all the components that make up your entrepreneurial perspective, recognizing that our list here is not exhaustive, these factors can be summed up in one word. Combining self reliance, appreciation of the risk of not having a steady paycheck, working all the time and then making the most of that time can be boiled down to one word that defines your perspective.

What is that word? Actually, it is a different word for different entrepreneurs. For some, the word is "serious." For some, it is "urgency." For others, it is "commitment." The word that goes through your mind may be completely different from these. It is important, however, to boil it down to just one word. You can easily wrap your mind around one word and then just change the context to fit your situation. That word will define your perspective. When it does, then you will see how you are different from those who do not work for themselves. For you, the word that might sum up your perspective might be "intense." For a person who works for someone else, the word that sums up his or her perspective might be "content" or "satisfied" or "comfortable." When you recognize that those words can never be used to describe your perspective, you will realize that you are very different from them.

CHAPTER 9
Is it Okay to Feel "Special?"

Well that is a cute question. The more recent connotations of the word may make you not want to be "special" but in the conventional definition of the word, it is a worthy question. We all like to feel special. Think about how your mother may have made you feel. Think about your first love. Think about the people who have loved you. In one way or another, many of them made you feel "special." However, in operating your own business, is it okay to feel "special?"

Feeling special basically means that you feel that you are different. Moreover, it implies that you have a feeling that you will not only be different, but that you have the capacity to do or be something extraordinary in the eyes of someone else. In developing and maintaining the attitude necessary to continue on in your small business, you need to feel that you have the ability to be extraordinary for yourself.

This does not mean that you should be egotistical. There is a difference between feeling that you are special and thinking that you are great and that everything revolves around you and your needs. Feeling special about yourself does not mean that you believe that your needs are more important than the needs of others. It means that you do not necessarily think that you are better than everybody else. In fact, people who recognize that they are special see themselves in terms of what they can do for others and not necessarily what they can do for themselves. In that way, feeling that you are "special" is a more noble proposition than you might have originally understood when I asked the question: "is it okay to feel 'special?"

An entrepreneur who feels that they are special believes that he or she can perform a service or manufacture a product for people in a way that is different from competitors and colleagues. It means that the entrepreneur sees himself or herself as being different from other people. Sometimes, the entrepreneur needs to feel that he or she is uniquely qualified to satisfy his or her customers. In some cases, it means that the entrepreneur feels that he or she can satisfy the customers in a unique manner that is very different from the entrepreneur's contemporaries.

It is important to recognize that entrepreneurs who feel that they are special have a focus on what they are capable of doing for others. The entrepreneur should not let the focus return to themselves so as to become egotistical about feeling special. No one really benefits from the politician who thinks that people should vote for him or her because she knows more than any body else and his or her way is the only way to benefit everybody. Feeling special should not allow you to develop a big head. All that feeling special should do is to reinforce your commitment to your customers. It should make you focus on being able to fulfill either the unique needs of your customers or to fulfill their needs in some unique manner.

As an example, if you are in the catering business and your company serves a dessert item that none of your competitors serve, then you are fulfilling a unique need for the customers who want that dessert. You may also be a caterer who has built special trucks that have on board ovens, microwaves, stoves and burners that allow you to serve food anywhere including places without kitchens. In this way, you might be the only caterer doing this and that makes you special in the way you are serving your customers.

The benefit of thinking of yourself as special becomes more clear as you think about it in terms of how your customers and clients view you. Once you feel special about what you have to offer, then you will begin to project that to your customers. So long as you believe it they will come to recognize it. Sometimes you will need to advertise it and sometimes you will need to merely let it naturally display itself. But, once customers get the message that what you have to offer is unique compared to your competitor, they will seek you out because you are special.

So, once you see yourself as different or special compared to your competition and once you project that image to your customers, then when choosing who to give their business to, they will recognize that you are different from your competitors.

This is the big deal. It is what you strive to be. It is the whole enchilada, the primo taco and the grand prize of all that you do in business. You want your customers to feel that you are special and unique and therefore "different" from your competitors. Things that are different stand out. When you stand out, people choose you over others. In business, making customers choose you over your competition is what competing is all about.

And, it all starts with feeling special about yourself.

CHAPTER 10
A Costs-Benefit Analysis of Perfection

In the development of your "entrepreneurial attitude" you need to be driven. You need to strive to perform as best you can. You need to push yourself to plateaus that exceed your own expectations of yourself. But, do you need to strive for perfection? Perfection is not typically possible time after time in every situation. The odds are against always being able to be perfect. But, even if we accept the fact that we cannot be perfect all the time, is it worth shooting for in the first place?

This is a tough question because not striving for perfection seems contrary to striving to do the best you can. There is no contradiction however. Trying to do your best and trying to be perfect are two different things. Unless you are perfect, you cannot strive to be perfect. You can strive to do your best however. Whereas performing perfectly by definition implies that your attempt allows for no margin for error, you cannot operate on the premise that you will never make a mistake.

The problems with the idea that you can be perfect are two-fold. First, it is unrealistic to think that you can always achieve a perfect result. Your ego would be too big to perform at that level realistically. Moreover, anyone who believes that they are perfect invites a harsh visit from fate. Your attitude becomes such that either fate will show you that you are imperfect, or, people and entities will conspire to bring about your demise to show you that you are not perfect. Realistically, therefore, perfection is undermined by fate or the greater ability of others individually or in groups to beat you. One way or another, you will be brought down a peg from the lofty plateau of perfection.

Second, there is pressure that one puts on oneself when trying to be perfect that undermines the attempt. Mentally, your brain tells you that perfection is not attainable and therefore, despite your best efforts, you end up making a stupid mistake. I see it all the time in golf. You hit a super drive on a par 5 and then you hit your second shot to within 18 inches of the hole. Then you miss the putt for eagle. What happened? The putt was the easiest part and yet it was the task that you did not perform perfectly. Golfers blame this on the golf gods when they really need to look at themselves. Is it possible that your mind forgot about your goal to be perfect? Is it possible that your mind deserted you in your commitment to be perfect? For whatever reason, after doing all the hard parts right, the smallest task to achieve perfection has added pressure. Why do our minds work like this? I do not know. I am asking. Call a shrink.

Anyway, the point is that thinking that you can be perfect is almost counterproductive to doing your best. So, left to strive for doing your best may lead you to striving to either always performing successfully or never making a mistake. Despite the fact that these are different things, different people define perfection as one of these two accomplishments.

Mistake Free "Perfection"

Sadly, we live in a world that, in certain professions, does not allow for mistakes. Doctors cannot screw up for fear that someone will suffer or die. Pharmacists cannot screw up for the same fear. Accountants and financial planners cannot screw up because to do so could jeopardize a client's money. Corporate directors and officers cannot screw up because to do so would jeopardize the shareholders' investment. Lawyers cannot screw up because to do so would jeopardize a client's rights, finances or family.

The worst part about all of this is that none of the aforementioned people can ever admit responsibility nor can they say that they are sorry if they do screw up. If they do, they will be crucified, or worse, they will be sued. And when they get sued, litigators make damn certain that the eventual punishment for the infraction is far more dire than the original infraction. You can almost hear the conversation: "hey I won the lottery!" "Oh yeah, that's nothing, my surgeon left a sponge in me that I never even felt and my lawyer told me that I'm gonna get millions!" That is where you have the problem of course. The person never felt the sponge but still will reap a great deal of money for their alleged suffering. And the surgeon has to pay rather than merely apologizing and fixing what happened.

The new standard for professionals is perfection based on the idea of having made no mistakes. Or, if you do make a mistake, you can have a minor failure with an excuse that results in no liability. It seems impossible that so many people have to live with having to be perfectly mistake free for every customer, client and patient. They have to be successful for each otherwise they open themselves up to lawsuits for malpractice.

It makes me wonder why anyone ever becomes a professional. Think about it. Look at Tiger Woods. Did he win every tournament that he entered? Is there anyone waiting to sue him if he misses the cut? (Well maybe Nike would be upset that no one will see the Swoosh on his shirt during the weekend rounds but Nike will not sue him). I realize that he performs brilliantly under pressure but if he had to always be perfect for every tournament and could not possibly risk any mistakes, would he continue to do it? Next time Tiger faces a six foot putt for par and it could cost him a couple hundred thousand if he misses it, ask him if he would rather have someone's life or life savings on the line. "Hey Tiger, if you miss this putt, someone other than you is going to lose hundreds of thousands of dollars they do not have. Or, if you screw up, a guy could get the wrong medication and die. Or, if you screw up, a guy might not get custody of his kids and they will never know the type of relationship that you had with your father. Well, go ahead, putt!" When Phil Mickelson choked on the final hole at Winged Foot and lost the United States Open, the world felt sorry for him. Maybe they thought he was a fool. Maybe they agreed with him that he was an idiot. But, if a surgeon screws up during the fifth complicated emergency surgery that he or she had that day, then no one feels sorry for the surgeon. No one feels that they were merely an idiot. The loved ones of the patient feel that the surgeon is a villain. The surgeon now owes somebody.

It begs the question. Why would anyone operate a business in a profession where you have to be perfect all the time?   Why operate a business where you had to strive for mistake free perfection?

The only way it can be done in these situations is for the individual to redefine their image of perfection. This does not seem obvious to most logical people but to lawyers it makes perfect sense. All you need to do is lower the standard of how you define "perfection" and then perfection is attainable. They could say that Sammy Sosa had a perfect career. Some would argue that. Strictly speaking however, perfect would imply that he got at least a base hit for every at bat. His average would be 1.000. He did not do that. Now, if we redefine perfection and take out a strict interpretation, Sammy's career can be seen as perfect. If we say that he was significantly better than others and that is all he needed to do then he might have attained perfection. This is how certain professionals cope with having to be perfect. Surgeons merely say to themselves, the overwhelming majority of my cases, compared to those of my peers, have been successful. I have successfully avoided any malpractice suits and therefore, I have been perfect. Whether you can live with the moving target of what is perfection in your particular profession is for you alone to decide. For anyone's part, the best thing to do is to either redefine perfection or agree that perfection time after time is not attainable and then set a sufficiently high standard for yourself.

But what if you want to be perfect in your business in the true unadulterated definition of the word and your business is selling truck tires. You do not have the malpractice issues and seriousness of consequences that other professionals deal with for making mistakes that result in imperfection. If you fail to get the tires to a customer on time, no one is going to die necessarily. Can you strive to be the perfect tire supplier?

Uninterrupted Success Perfection

Perfection in the form of always being successful is nice to think about but, in your small business, it might be too costly to even try to achieve. Perfection of this sort, and attempts at trying to reach that perfection, by necessity implies that an extraordinary effort was applied to the performance of every task to guarantee success for every customer. When we consider that the effort was "extraordinary" we are acknowledging that the effort was not merely ordinary. If we need to apply more effort than any task needs in performing every task then we have wasted effort. You cannot always put in more effort than any particular task needs. You would never have time to always put in more effort than needed in order to guarantee the perfection or successful completion of every task.

Time is interesting. If I had all the time in the world, I could accomplish anything. I could study every question and read every case and always know every answer. With all the time in the world, I could be perfect. I always wondered if the difference between God and man was that God never had to watch a clock. The Guy who is making all those beautiful sunsets and snow flakes and mountains must not have been worried about finishing on time. His work is just too good to have been under that kind of pressure. Or, did pressure have something to do with it?

Lack of all the time in the world is the trick for all of us. Maybe even for Him. Trying to be perfect under time constraints is exhilarating for some. When time comes into play, then your efforts have to be tailored to the individual situation and your efforts have to be perfect. When time comes into play, you usually do not have the luxury of fully investigating every consequence of a decision. Yet, if your decision making must be perfect without all the time in the world to see if it is the right decision, there is some element of excitement in that. The problem, of course, is that without all the time in the world and the ability to investigate every possible outcome of a decision, you will have to rely on luck.

The law of averages holds that you cannot always be perfectly lucky. You may be lucky a vast majority of the time but to have perfect luck is impossible. Moreover, in a realistic assessment of your attitude in operating your business, you should know better than to count on your luck. To always be successful time and time again will by necessity require that forces beyond your control will always help you to succeed and never prevent your success. To think that fate will never work against you even if you do your best is unrealistic. Some element of being successful time and time again will always rely, to some extent, on being lucky.

The Cost-Benefit Analysis of trying to Achieve Perfection

So all of this being said, absent all the time in the world and absent perfect luck, is it worth trying to be perfect all the time? The answer lies in the cost-benefit analysis of perfection. Does the cost in time and effort to perform a task justify doing it perfectly? Is there a sufficient benefit in perfection to justify an extraordinary effort and cost? In business the answer is typically: no. Perfection is expensive. As it should be. As you think about it, do you really need perfection? Is there a lesser standard you could reasonably attempt to attain that would justify the cost of your time and efforts better than shooting for perfection?

The lesser standard, by definition, implies that perfection is being compromised. Some lesser target that is more in line with what can reasonably be achieved day in and day out becomes your focus. The lesser target can be attained in the time constraints that you have. The lesser target does not have to rely upon perfect luck for you to be confident that you can achieve the goal.

What is this "lesser target?" Well, if we do not play games with the definition of perfection it is a little easier to explain. Assuming that perfect means completely without flaw and to the highest level of achievement, then our lesser target can have flaws and be below the highest level of achievement. We focus on a target that is the best that we can do under the time constraints we have.

Provided that we accept our time constraints, the "lesser target" from perfection becomes "the best we can do." What does it take to do your best? That is the question you have to ask yourself. This is where some people running businesses fail. Every individual has a different definition of the "best that they can do." Businesses fail either because the operator does not have the ability to perform or because the operator consistently performs at a level that is less than their full abilities.

It becomes a matter of recognizing one's capabilities and then either performing up to those capabilities or not. In assessing one's capabilities, people tend to either over or under estimate themselves. We see this all the time. The personal service person, like a doctor, who is always running late for appointment throughout the day because he believes he can see 40 patients in a day. Or the truck driver who turns down a third profitable delivery assignment because he has two jobs already that should take three hours a piece but he believes it will take him a full eight hours to do both.

In assessing your capabilities you need to look at your history. If you are constantly running late on assignments, then you need to schedule more time for what you need to accomplish. If you are always finishing your work day early, then you need to schedule more work for each particular day. The important thing to remember is to assess over time how you perform. Then once you have performed that assessment, ask yourself, am I doing my best?

To perform at your best, you need to commit mentally to doing everything you can within reasonable time constraints to perform the task successfully. Define success for the task at hand. Perfection may not be possible or cost effective so do not equate perfection with success. Success should be defined as customer or client's satisfaction. This, of course, will depend upon the reasonableness of the customer or client. If the client needs his grass cut then he should not use a laser to check the uniform height of the blades after you have cut it. Such action on his part makes him unreasonable unless, he is paying you about $1,000.00 per quarter acre. Why anyone would pay that begs the question of their reasonableness however. No one needs that much perfection in the cutting of their lawn. But if the guy is paying you $75.00 to cut the lawn then it should be cut, it should probably be edged and you should clean up and dispose of the clippings for him. If $75.00 is a reasonable price, then you should exert the effort reasonably necessary to cut the lawn to the customer's satisfaction.

The foregoing example leads to the final part of your analysis. You need to ask, what am I charging for my efforts? You need to set an hourly rate for yourself. This is one of the best ways to align "the best that you can do" with reasonable customer satisfaction. If your time is worth $25.00 per hour, then the customer who hires you to do a four hour job should expect to pay $100.00. But, if the customer says he is willing to pay $50.00 and you know that it is a four hour job, then you already have a clue as to that customer's potential level of satisfaction. You now have to decide whether you want to discount your time to half of what you have determined it is worth in order to try to satisfy this particular customer. Why should you commit four hours to this customer?

The answer is: you should not commit to taking this job. If you do then you will either be trying to be perfect in taking every job that comes your way, or, you will take the job and do less than your best because you resent not being paid what you feel you are worth. The point is that you should determine what will be a successful outcome for any particular customer. Then you should determine what your time is worth and calculate how much time is necessary to achieve success for the customer. If the customer is willing to pay what you quote, then you should fully commit to achieving a successful outcome for that customer within the time constraints that you proposed.

Perfection in the form of not making any mistakes or guaranteeing success is not part of this formula. Success for the customer as a result of you doing the best you can at a rate that is within what you believe your time is worth is the only formula to consider and should be the only goal. That is what you should strive for and, that is what should form the basis of your entrepreneurial attitude.

CHAPTER 11
Saving for Rainy Day
What a Crock of Crap

Do you recall all those old sayings and platitudes and wives' tales and other stuff you always heard such as: save your pennies for a rainy day? Does it make you sick to think of them? Me too. One of the attitude adjustments you need to make in business is to not be so simple minded as to buy into all the crap. Unless it motivates you in some way, do not buy into it. It is a slippery slope. (Is anyone counting the overused clichés in this book?).

Anyway, in most small businesses you cannot save your pennies for a rainy day because it seems like every day is a rainy day. It never stops raining long enough for you to save your pennies. Besides, why would anyone think that you could collect more pennies on a sunny day?

What does all this have to do with entrepreneurial attitude? Easy, an entrepreneur needs to feel free to question conventional thinking from time to time. How do you develop the mind set to question conventional wisdom? It all starts with the right attitude.

Mind you, the attitude that we are discussing is not merely a form of pessimism. It does not mean that you need to be surly or rude. It does not imply that you need to be sarcastic or ornery. It certainly does not mean that you need to be cynical or overly critical of others.

Being any one of the foregoing things makes you an asshole and not an entrepreneur. Take it from an asshole. But still, to develop the right entrepreneurial attitude, you need to question things and accept fewer things on shear faith. So without being an asshole, you need to be inquisitive. Maybe, if you do not get answers to your questions then, and only then, do you become demanding. If that does not work, become an asshole.

If you do not ask questions, then people will believe that they can treat you like the type of people who go away once you tell them, "save your pennies for a rainy day." Entrepreneurs need to have others take them seriously. In order to be taken seriously, you cannot let others perceive that you are shallow. Shallow people can be put off with clichés and platitudes.

That is not you. You are a thinking individual who is willing to pay the price for information and answers so long as your requests are taken seriously.

In addition, you need to get over being embarrassed about asking questions. If something does not make sense, ask a question. If something seems too simple, ask why. If someone is not giving you a straight answer, ask again. Politely tell them that you need an appropriate response. Do not accept anything short of a genuine answer.

Entrepreneurs cannot be shrinking violets (add this to the cliché count). If the meek shall inherit the earth then they will get it after everyone else has used and abused it. Entrepreneurs cannot be meek and cannot be perceived as willing to meagerly walk away from people who do not have time for them. They need to assert themselves at least enough to show people that they are there. Here is one more cliché: do you know about the squeaky wheel?

The simple act of asserting oneself should not turn you into an ass however. People do not long to do business with assholes. Often times, being an asshole gets you the worst service and poor treatment if anyone wants to do business with you at all. Asserting yourself without being pompous is what being an entrepreneur is all about. You need to stand out but you cannot be conspicuously nasty about it. It is difficult to balance these competing forces but it most be done. Striking that balance is an essential element of the entrepreneurial attitude.

I had known George for about three years after he had opened his marketing and promotions business. After about three years in business, he found himself in need of a cash restructuring. Essentially, he had run into short term cash flow problems and needed to work something out with the bank in order to handle these issues as they came up. He had studied different banks and different programs including lines of credit. He was confused. He asked me for help and I told him all of the problems I had always had with cash flow. He immediately recognized my limitations and decided that he would seek answers elsewhere. I suggested one of the local banks. He thanked me for the advice and he gave it a try.

George went to the local bank and met, I kid you not, Steve Slick. Mr. Slick was, of course, a vice-president at that branch because anyone who has worked in any bank for more than four hours gets to be a vice-president. It is a sad state of affairs that the banking industry today lacks sufficient creativity to invent new titles other than just calling everyone a vice-president. I once saw a guy mopping the floor at a bank and his badge identified him as the "Vice-President of Premises Maintenance." If you were to call a bank and reach the switch board and then ask to speak to a vice-president, the operator could either take the call herself or connect you with virtually anyone else at the bank. I guess that is the reward for working in such a low paying industry. Maybe they tell people at the interview, "you know, we don't pay much but if you stay past lunch on your first day, we will make you a vice president of something. Tell that to your mother."

So here was George, seeking advice from Steve Slick. Mr. Slick, who might have been legally old enough to purchase alcohol for the first time as recently as that morning, briefly explained different programs and packages. He described one loan after another. He smiled a lot acting as if George understood. Mr. Slick seemed to be hoping that at least one of them understood what he was saying because he did not. George identified the cash flow circumstances and Mr. Slick told him, without blinking an eye, "you know, maybe we could discuss ways in which you can learn to save for a rainy day."

What happened next made me more proud of George than I have been of almost any client I have ever had the pleasure of serving. George had done his homework and with Mr. Slick's off hand comment, George knew that he was not being taken seriously. So George politely asked questions. He asked about rate formulas for adjustable lines of credit. He asked about capital and asset pledges. He asked about financial reports, projections and balance statements. He asked about personal guarantees and UCC filings. Mr. Slick could not answer any of George's questions. George figured that he could not.

George is a pretty humble guy if you ever met him. Everyone likes him. He is kind and generous. So it is not surprising to recognize that George was not asking his questions to embarrass Mr. Slick. If you knew George, you would know that he was not trying to show off what he knew. He was trying to get answers for what he did not know. In doing so, he demonstrated to Mr. Slick that he wished to have real answers to his questions. He demonstrated that he was a business man, and even though his business was small, he was sophisticated enough to understand finance.

Most importantly, George showed the bank that he had an entrepreneurial attitude. He expressed himself in a professional and businesslike manner. He showed that he wanted to discuss real issues and obtain real information not merely off handed comments like "you ought to learn how to save for a rainy day."

Mr. Slick's boss, the "Vice-President of Vice-President Development," happened to be passing by Mr. Slick's desk as George was asking his questions. He was impressed with George. He was more impressed with George than Mr. Slick actually. He interrupted Mr. Slick's less than slick presentation and immediately took George to his office where he had a more detailed discussion of George's needs. He apologized for the inexperience of Mr. Slick and he offered George tickets to a baseball game. It seemed that Mr. Slick's boss recognized that George was the type of guy the bank wanted as a customer and he went out of his way to accommodate George.

George declined the baseball game tickets but did eventually open a line of credit account with the bank specifically tailored to his company's needs. To this day, the bank considers George one of its best, if not necessarily one of its biggest, customers. The difference is George's attitude. The bank knows that George is a nice man who does not want to deal with B.S. He is real. His needs are real. His business is a real concern and his attitude reflects that. His attitude conveys to the people at the bank and everywhere else with whom he does business that George is worthy of real respect and not merely polite clichés.

So as you sit behind your desk wondering what is the right attitude to show your customers, suppliers, lenders and anyone you do business with, think about George. Think about what you need to do to develop the type of attitude necessary to show that you are real and not a cliché. Show people that you are a nice guy but not the kind of nice guy who finishes last. You are a nice guy who is doing business and realizes that you cannot finish last.

CHAPTER 12
Can I be my own Boss?

Just the other day, my wife heard a commercial on the radio about opening a new business and it made her think. As a result of that commercial, she asked me, "do you think that I should be my own boss?" I felt compelled to answer her honestly and so I did. "Actually honey, I think that you should. The way that you boss me around all the time has given you more than enough experience being a boss. Also, it might be nice for you to see what it is like to have to work for you."

So here I am at two o'clock in the morning for the third night in a row unable to get comfortable on our couch and realizing that some people, such as spouses, do not wish to be told the truth. Realizing the damage I had done to my standing in the household, I also recognized that my brief conversation with my wife does illustrate a point. Can any of us be our own boss?

Once again, I return to my legal training in making a qualified answer to the question. The simple answer is: of course some of us can be our own boss. And you can even add to the answer: people do it successfully all the time. The qualifications are where the real answer lies however. Those qualifications are that SOME people can do it and only SOME are successful. So if we all agree that some people can successfully be their own boss, then we need to address what makes some people successful at it and others not so successful. Then we can ask the final question, if we cannot be successful at it, can we be our own boss?

In future chapters we will talk about wearing different hats in our business. We will discuss the differences between officers, directors and shareholders. We will discuss what partners do. We have already discussed the difference between ourselves as entrepreneurs and ourselves as employees in previous chapters. In this chapter, however, we will discuss whether you can be both an entrepreneur and an employee.

The phrase "working for yourself" has difference connotations. The connotations depend upon which word jumps out at you. For those who focus on the word "working" the phrase implies that you are employed.

Perhaps, to some, it means that you are in a servitude. But, in any event, it implies that you are obligated to work.

For those who focus on the word "yourself" the phrase implies that you are the boss. You are not answerable to someone else. You are self sufficient and potentially self sustaining. It also means that you are overseeing someone. Someone has to perform work for you.

Depending upon which word you focus on as you think about the phrase, you can recognize the necessity of having to accept that "working for yourself" means that you are both the employee and the employer. Adding both connotations together, it means that you are obligated to work for yourself and that you have no one to answer to as you are the boss.

Now ask yourself what kind of employee you are. Do you work hard or do you do just enough to get by? Do you take time off and show little or no commitment to the goals of management? Are you driven by your own sense of accomplishment or are you driven by a task master boss? Do you resent working or to relish it?

Then you need to ask yourself what kind of employer you are. Do you set unreal expectations for your staff? Are you sensitive to their needs? Do you instruct them patiently? Do you find realistic ways to motivate them or do you merely threaten? Are you a good and effective leader? As an employer, are you loved, understood, despised, respected etc.? Or are you a sucker, an ass, a bitch (bastard), a moron, etc.?

After thinking about all of this, you can bring yourself to the main question: Am I the kind of employee who can work for a boss like me? When you answer that, then you can answer the question as to whether you can be your own boss.

I knew two people who were faced with this question when the company they had been working for announced that it was going out of business. They each decided that it was time to try to make it on their own in the wake of the sudden demise of their employer. Each would have benefitted from assessing what type of boss and employee they would be for themselves however.

First, there was Gwen. When Gwen first told me that she wanted to open her own computer and software consulting business I was happy for her. Her plan made sense. She had a degree in computer science and had been working in the software development department of her former firm for many years. She had fixed many different types of applications and equipment. She had the technical knowledge. Gwen was also very driven. She had advanced through the ranks of her prior jobs and she had a very good reputation for being a hard-working employee.

Cliff, on the other hand, was not as driven. He was pretty laid back. He had a reputation for being somewhat of a party guy. Although everyone knew that he had great natural skill and knowledge, he was looked at by many as a "slacker." He did what he could to get by but usually nothing more. He was at best a lump of undeveloped talent. Nevertheless, he too wanted to open his own business doing consulting regarding computers and networks.

Now for those of you expecting a tortoise and hare analogy please remember that I deal in reality. The happy ending that the tortoise looks for in beating the hare does not happen in reality. The hare can screw off and he will probably still win.

At their former firm, both Gwen and Cliff had occasions to supervise others. As you might expect, Gwen was somewhat hard driving and expected the most from her underlings. Cliff, on the other hand, was the classic idiot boss who did not delegate well but was well liked by the people working for him.

When each of them opened their respective businesses, they had no money for employees. As a result, each was going to work for themselves. Gwen went to work immediately. She developed every type of system in the world to run the business. She researched every expense. She purchased all the best equipment and she made sure that she got the best deal. She acquired sophisticated, but reasonably priced, office space. She developed complex databases for client contacts and other sources for her business. She hired one of the best attorneys she could. She remains one of my very favorite clients.

Meanwhile, Cliff was Cliff. He took his time getting started. He was not much of a boss and even less of an employee so he really did not push himself. He was keeping receipts in a shoe box. His office was a small portion of his apartment. His X-Box was his major business purchase.

Over time, I found myself to be meeting with Gwen quite often as she tried to get the business off the ground. Always efficient, she was on time for every meeting and she took notes from every consultation.

Despite her best efforts however, some problems arose for her. Gwen began to become flustered with the business she had founded. Despite her systems and attention to every detail, she always felt inadequate. She was very critical of herself despite the fact that she was working 75-90 hours per week. Overall, when I asked her how business was she would answer that she was not satisfied. She felt that she could always do more and that she had accomplished very little.

Meanwhile, Cliff did not come to see me as often. He seemed to get lucky with a number of things. He stumbled into a major company that needed extensive IT work and despite (if not because of) his arrogance and laissez faire attitude, he got the work. He could never get himself to work on time for the client. He never gave it a second thought however. He never showed anyone that he cared that much. He never got down on himself about it. When I asked him how business was he said that he had no real complaints. His billing was behind because he never got around to it but otherwise, he was fine.

When I was visiting Gwen in the hospital after her nervous breakdown, I felt the need to ask her what happened. She told me that she felt that she was always a failure. She never felt that she had met her own expectations. She felt that she worked hard but that she did not succeed to the extent that she wanted.

Meanwhile, when Cliff got audited he genuinely seemed sorry for not forcing himself to keep better records. He ended up paying hefty penalties to the IRS for lost receipts and poor record keeping. He did not let it get to him however. He had made a lot of money on his own despite himself. He admitted that he could have made more money but that he was making as much as would make him happy for now.

The point of the story is that Gwen, despite being a great employee, was also a difficult boss and she wanted perfection in herself that eventually unraveled her. She was too driven as an employer to accept herself as an employee. She felt dissatisfied as a result of being too hard on herself.

Cliff, on the other hand, probably needed to be a better employee. But, in order to be one, he needed to push himself by being a better employer. Overall, he was not dissatisfied he just was not getting the job done. He was also not realizing his potential. But, because he was not much of a boss, he never set the bar higher. He was a complacent boss who did not push himself.

So which is better? Neither really. Cliff is still in business but he still is likely to get audited again and again and he will never really fulfill his full potential. Gwen left the business and married one of her doctors. She now has a perfect family, perfect house and seems perfectly happy after taking her psych meds. Off her meds, she will admit that she is not happy.

The point is that you have to accept a very simple principal. You need to be both employer and employee in order to be your own boss. Unless you can do both and unless you know how you will be as both a boss and employee, you cannot answer the question whether you can be your own boss.

How do you become the right type of employer for yourself as an employee? Looking at the two examples I have mentioned, I would have had only a few suggestions. These suggestions are based on experience and creative thinking more than a specific formula. You will find that creative thinking is probably the best way to answer the question for yourself.

In Gwen's case, I would have suggested that she look outside of herself for advice and an objective opinion. She should have decided which role, boss or employee, was more important and then she should have looked for an opinion from someone else regarding her fulfillment of her employee duties. If someone had told her not to be so hard on herself and had advised her of a set group of specific standards to set for herself as an employee, then she could have dealt with herself as an employee. For example, I would have told her that she should set her maximum hours per week. She should have certain to do's on her list and that she should consider herself successful once she completed all of the to do's. Finally, I would have told her to have someone else monitor the "to do" list to determine if it was reasonable. Essentially, I was telling her to get an outside opinion to determine whether she was being fair to herself.

With Cliff. I think he should have had asked customers to give him performance appraisals. He should have asked them to give him suggestions as to what might have made his services better. Then, if he cared about the customers and his business, he could have used those suggestions and performance appraisals as guidelines for himself as the boss to give to himself as the employee.

The proposals I have made here are not the only ones that could be made to either of these two very distinct people. As a prospective entrepreneur, I feel certain that anyone seriously reading this book could think of other ways to help people become better at being a boss for himself or herself as an employee. If you could strike the right balance and find the most effective way to deal with yourself as both employee and boss then you can become successful at it as only SOME can.

CHAPTER 13
Your Goal should be Success!
There is no joke in that. When the Work Gets Overwhelming, Remember that Goal.

I should point out that I am a casual observer of successful and less than successful people. You will notice that I have not referred to them as "failures." We cannot call them failures because of political correctness issues. It seems that political correctness is a way of side stepping the first amendment. I guess that you can have any free speech you want so long as your opinion or how you phrase it does not offend people. I guess it is offensive to refer to some people as "failures." The very implications of that word when used to refer to people, much less people who have tried to operate their own business, is so profoundly upsetting that the utterance of the word is disgusting. After all, success is so relative.

As an example, consider those people who file multiple bankruptcies. I should point out that I mean no offense to the many people who file bankruptcy as a result of overwhelming circumstances such as significant medical problems etc. and who have no choice. Those people are not failures as much as they are unlucky. I understand and respect the difference as do most reasonably intelligent people.

But, let us consider the bankruptcy filers who are merely trying to avoid their creditors and have no conscience about filing bankruptcy. To them, success is relative. Just because they have filed bankruptcy last year and now find themselves waiting for the next six years for their first opportunity to file again does not mean that they are failures. It just means that relative to people who are trying to pay their creditors and who are doing so through hard work and thrift, they are not as successful. But that is okay these days because we live in a world that gives the last place little league team a trophy for "trying."

Personally, I can think of no greater source of embarrassment than to have a trophy on your shelf that indicates that you "tried hard" but still came in last. Why in the hell does this society celebrate defeat. I would almost prefer a trophy that indicated that I totally screwed off and did not try hard then one that stands as a monument to the fact that despite my best efforts, I failed.

Here is my very simple point. Society is that screwed up. You are in your own business and you cannot afford to be that screwed up. For you, success and failure need to be clearly defined. Success is not on a sliding scale of some sort and it most certainly is not relative. If you begin to feel that success is relative then you are in trouble.

At first, when success is relative it is okay. You compare yourself to people who are pretty good at things. If you do as good as they do things, then you are probably successful. But then, if you do not do as good, success becomes relative. You start building up excuses as to why you are not as successful as the people you once compared yourself to. Then, you tell yourself, "relative" to them, I am successful. Or worse, you compare yourself to people who are significantly less successful than the people you once idolized. You then have fully embraced the concept that success is relative. You tell yourself that I am successful. I am not as successful as the best people in the industry but, relative to some of the total butt losers that I am willing to compare myself to in order to feel better, I am successful.

To further explain the point, I often talk about this imaginary baseball team that I follow. They play in the fantasy league, I call them the Chicago Cubs. This imaginary team has not won a World Series in almost a century. They have not been to the World Series in over half a century. Yet, I and so many people with whom I share a passion for this team still think that 2003 was a successful year for our imaginary Cubs. That year they went deep into the playoffs needing only one win to go to the World Series. As in all good fantasies there was some unbelievable series of events that stopped them. They fell short by having their two best pitchers lose back to back games against a team lead by one of Moses' contemporaries who was a last minute replacement for a team that had fired its manager. You see, I told you that this was all imaginary. The Cubs would have been on the way to the World Series but this guy grabbed a fowl ball from the stands and despite having the two best pitchers in baseball pitching for almost a game and a half after that, the Cubs lost the series that would have put them in the Big One. So you see, the Cubs really were successful. It is just that this guy caught that fowl ball. Relative to what the Cubs had to deal with, however, they were successful. The Cubs finished in front of other teams like the imaginary Pittsburgh Pirates and the imaginary Cincinnati Reds. So only if you are so focused on something as trivial as being World Champions at least once in a century can you think of the Cubs as failures. Otherwise, relative to lots of other teams, all of whom have been to the World Series, the Cubs are hugely successful. You see, it is all relative.

Here is the point. Once success becomes relative you become complacent. Once you become complacent, failure happens. Once you have one failure it becomes easier to accept the next failure. Before long you do not care.

That is why you need to have one goal in business. That goal is success.

Now I am certainly not going to define what success should be for you. Only you as an individual entrepreneur can define success for yourself. In that regard, you can elect to set the bar as high or as low as you wish. The most important thing is that once you define what you consider to be successful, then you should strive to achieve. If you fail, do not merely accept it. Do not give yourself a trophy for "trying hard." If anything, tell yourself that you did not try hard and that by trying hard next time, you will succeed.

In my previous book I turned this into a pep talk. I am not doing that in this book. In this book I am talking to people who are already in business. Maybe it has become overwhelming and they are confused. Maybe things have not gone well and they have become depressed. Maybe things have gotten so out of control that they cannot fathom getting back on the horse and pushing for a success in the wake of such despair.

To these people I say: FOCUS!!! Get your mind back on your goal. If you think about or focus on failure, it becomes a self fulfilling prophecy. If you focus on your success, then who knows how far you can go. As you think about your success, consider how it will feel to move from where you are to the point where you achieve your goals. Think about how good you will feel about yourself as you do not give up but instead deal with your circumstances and then find a way to fulfill your goal. There is a benefit to that feeling. That is the stuff that you should get a trophy for.

The other benefit from focusing on your goal and overcoming

adversity is that by doing so, you will develop confidence. So that the next time it becomes overwhelming you can say to yourself, I got through tough times before. You can then believe in yourself to do it again.

Notwithstanding anything I have said already, this book comes from my observations of both types of people. I share those observations with the reader in the form of advice so that you think that I am a successful guy also. I do spend a considerable amount of time observing people who are both successful and people who fail. One I observe in the mirror almost everyday. I have had my share of failures and I have seen myself succeed. I have steadily learned over time not to fear my failures. Failure preys upon those who fear it. I have learned instead that I do not wish to accept my failures. I have also learned that I truly enjoy when I am successful at things.

What I have learned about failure is that you should never let one failure lead to another. If you make a mistake, learn from it. Do not repeat mistakes. Do not discount a mistake as merely bad luck. Assess the mistake and the situation. If you could do something different that might result in success in the wake of a past failure, then do it. If you want the basketball to go in the hoop, aim better. If you are not getting it to the basket, throw harder. Do not merely do the same thing that you did last time hoping that the wind will take it. Do not merely say, well my last shot did not go in and that was unlucky. Try, try again does not mean that you should do the same thing the exact same way over and over again and then rely upon luck. Luck is shy. It does not come to those looking for it or relying upon it.

You can also pull success out of failure. What you learned in your last failed attempt may teach you what you need to know for your next successful try.

CHAPTER 14
Finding your Place in the Universe

As you operate your new business, there will be times when you need to consider your place in the universe. Actually, more important than your place in the universe is figuring out where you fit in the universe. Without getting too spiritual or existential, you need to figure out what role you fulfill in your business and what role your business fulfills in your industry.

This is a good time for a question on your part. Here is your question. "Why?"

That is a good question.

Your role in your business is important to think about and define from time to time because it helps you to address the needs of your business. For example, if everyone is sitting around, you may need to exert some authority. You may need to be the boss. You might need to assume this role. You may need to be the motivator. You might need to be the person who provides direction. You might need to be the example for the employees. You might need to be the comic relief.

No matter what role you might need to fulfill, you need to step back from time to time to think about it.

The same holds true for your business. It is all too easy to get into a rut and forget to think about what role your particular company fits in your industry. Maybe you have more stock than your competitors so you are the place that always has what people are looking for. Or maybe you are the most on time delivery company in your area. Maybe you are the most knowledgeable company in the market. Maybe your company is the rock in the industry that has been the place everyone knows about because it has been there forever.

Do not get confused. This is not about finding your niche. It is more about developing perspective. More importantly, this chapter is all about maintaining perspective. That perspective starts by developing an understanding of your business's place in the universe. Once that understanding is developed, you need to be able to never lose touch with that understanding. As those of you in business for yourselves have no doubt come to know, things in business change fast. Things that you could rely upon at one time cannot be relied upon forever. Large companies go in an out of business. Small companies go in and out of business. Industries crop up and disappear. Fads come and go. Some things stagnate while others are in constant flux. Unless you have a clear understanding of where your business is and where it fits into the entire picture, things could get out of control for you. Worse yet, you could miss opportunities or create situations that will result in your eventual downfall.

Your question of course is "how did perspective become so important?" If you are expecting me to say that it was always important, well then I have a surprise for you. Perspective has always been somewhat important but it has not always been as important as it has become since the early 1990's. What changed? The widened consumer and commercial use of the internet has dramatically increased the availability of the most precious commodity in the world: information. Add to that cable television, increased talk radio stations, cellular phone availability and use and you can begin to grasp the point.

The truth is that more information is available about your business and your competitors than ever. That being the case, it is important to have an identity for your business. Perspective comes from recognizing that identity.

Once again, this is not about having a niche. You do not need a unique identity. You could have an identity that is the same as ten or twenty of your competitors. If there is enough demand for your products or services to support you and ten to twenty other businesses exactly like yours, that is fine. What is important is that you recognize that you are in a business that is not distinct from your competitors. Maintaining that perspective will allow you to assess changes in the industry and react to those changes accordingly. For example, if the industry is in decline, sooner or later your business will suffer along with your competition. You need to understand your business's place in the industry to determine if long term survival is possible or if you need to branch into another industry.

Another consideration in this example is recognizing that if you and twenty competitors all do the same thing then how much of a market is necessary to keep all of you profitable? Suppose a major technological advancement comes along and it allows one of your competitors to produce more product at significantly lower prices. Now the market is flocking to him or her. Soon you and your other fellow competitors invest in the same technology to make yourselves more productive in order to compete. Now the price of your product is plummeting and profits for you and all the competitors who invested in technology are struggling to survive. Before long, the bottom falls out and you and all your competitors are floundering and in need of a bail out. There is a phrase that describes this example. It is called "the American Farm Industry in the Twentieth Century."

Being aware of your business's place in the universe does not guarantee that you will always react in the best manner so as to survive and prosper. But, it does increase the likelihood that you will at least react.

Arty was one of those business owners who never developed perspective. Arty was satisfied to just live and let live as far as business was concerned. He never assessed where his business fit into the world. He never really understood where it fit into his industry. For years he sailed along without developing that understanding and for years he was fine. Then all at once, things changed.

Arty had been selling car care cleaning products to retailers for years. His inventory had never changed in all that time. His way of selling had never changed in all that time. His sources of supply had never changed. If you had asked Arty about his competitors he could confirm that he had some but he had never met any of them. He could not recall any of their names. He could never tell you what the total gross sales was for the industry or what his local market share was. Things had always been going well so Arty never questioned anything. He had no innate curiosity. In Arty's case, it seemed that he was afraid to ask these questions for fear of tipping over his own apple cart. Now I wish I could say that Arty was an extreme case but sadly, as I have observed over these many years, he was not. Lots of business owners are like Arty. They have no idea what place their business holds in the universe.

If you are thinking that some tragic event is just around the corner for Arty from the way I set up this story, then you need to keep reading. This story turns out different from what you might be expecting.

Anyway, Arty was contacted one day by a young man who was interested in breaking into the car care cleaning business. The man came to see Arty from out of the blue and Arty agreed to have lunch with him. The man was impressed by how little Arty knew about his own company. During lunch, the man asked Arty if he had any plans of retiring and if Arty would consider selling the business when he did. Arty expressed that, for the right price, he would consider it. The man requested a price. Arty, thinking that he was being shrewd, offered to sell the business for $350,000.00. Arty admitted that he was setting the price at more than $150,000.00 than he really wanted but he wanted bargaining room. Imagine how Arty felt when the man said, "I could probably raise that amount and buy the business from you, if you are serious?"

Happier than a cat that had swallowed a canary and hoping to get away with it, Arty told him to write up the papers. Arty went home and he and the Mrs. danced all night thinking that they had been dreaming and hoping that the kid was not pulling their leg. Never in a million years had both Arty and his wife thought the business was worth $350,000.00. They were ecstatic.

It was about four months after that that Arty came to see me. He had sold the business and received the full amount of $350,000.00. But Arty was not happy. He wanted to rescind the contract. Somehow in the months since he sold the business, Arty learned that it might have been more valuable than he had originally thought.

When Arty sold it, he did not realize that he had signed an exclusive distributor agreement with one of his vendors. That agreement had been signed when the vendor was just starting out. When the vendor started out, it gave exclusive distributor agreements that lasted ten years to attempt to woo middlemen businesses like Arty's. Arty had never looked at the agreement. He just signed it and began selling for the vendor. What Arty learned after he sold the business was that the vendor had been expanding and desperately wanted to get out of its exclusive agreements. The vendor was looking to make a major move in buying out its largest competitor in the industry. If the exclusive distributor agreement had remained in place, the vendor would have been giving Arty a monopoly over one of its major markets.

But alas, poor Arty had sold the business and had assigned his rights under that contract to the young man who bought the business. Arty learned that his buyer had negotiated a deal with the vendor whereby the vendor paid $200,000.00 cash to modify the exclusive agreement and to enter into a new long terms agreement worth about $700,000.00 in sales over the next ten years.

When Arty explained all of this to me during our initial consultation four months after the sale and when I charged him $175.00 to basically explain that there was nothing he could do, Arty began to cry. Should I have not charged him? Heck no. He should have hired a lawyer in the first place to look over the contract and what Arty was selling. So I let him cry and I charged him. After all, he still received $350,000.00. He had the money. Sorry Arty but it is bad news and you owe me $175.00. Better luck selling your next business.

I felt bad. The man was sobbing. So I tried to make him feel a little better. I advised him that he did have $350,000.00. It was a pretty nice nest egg. He explained that he wanted the $900,000.00 that his buyer would reap. I told him that it was not likely to happen. Arty had set the price without knowing anything about his own business. No court would say that the sale was unconscionable and therefore should have been rescinded because Arty set the price. Certainly if he had known more about his business and its place in the industry, he could have made significantly more than what he did. But Arty never bothered to check. Arty asked how his buyer came to know the real value of Arty's business. I told Arty that most of the information had been obtained over the internet. The young man had read an article about this vendor buying old distributor contracts. He then called to find out who the distributor was in Chicago. The vendor told him it was Arty. Lunch followed. You know the rest. When Arty began crying into the second hour of our consultation, I had to let him know that I would have to charge him for another hour if he persisted. I let him know that it would be cheaper to go cry at home.

I guess that I do not have to say "the moral of the story is . . ." because it is pretty plain. Knowing you business's place in the universe can be pretty important. In Arty's case, it cost him dearly. Arty's problem was not that he did not realize that he had the exclusive distributor agreement. Arty's problem was that he did not know anything about his own business. He had no idea that he had almost a 78% market share over his competitors.

He did not even realize the nature of his business's relationship with one of its suppliers. This lack of knowledge concerning his company's own identity led Arty to believe that it was worth less than $350,000.00. Meanwhile Art got legally hustled and he could do nothing about it. If you sell your old car to a dealer not knowing that you forgot you had a bag with $10,000.00 in cash in the trunk, chances are the dealer is not going to give you your money back when he finds it.

If Arty had ever assessed the business, this could have been avoided. But he did not and spilled milk tends to stain and stink. That is worth crying about.

Chapter 15
The Competitor's Attitude, Mental Toughness and Identifying with being an Asshole

No book about being an entrepreneur is complete without at least some reference to competition. Competition, in its many forms, needs to be analyzed and understood. For example, understanding competition in the business context requires recognizing both direct and indirect competition. Direct competition is a company doing the exact same thing as you. You sell nuts and bolts, they sell nuts and bolts so they are direct competition. But, if you sell nuts and bolts and they sell rivets then that might be indirect competition. Indirect competitors may be in a different industry that can produce products and services that can satisfy the needs and wants of your customer base that are not the same products and services that you provide.

Because this book is not intended to be like others, we do not look at competition in the context of strategy and execution. Our interest, as always, is to develop perspective. The perspective that we are focusing on has to do with an entrepreneur's personal assessment of his or herself as a competitor. Putting aside all the thoughts you can muster about your competitors in your industry, you need to determine what your feelings are about being a competitor yourself. You need to ask yourself, what kind of competitor am I? You will be amazed at how few times entrepreneurs ask themselves this very important question. But, you might not be shocked to learn that certain people who are true competitors know exactly how to answer this question. Do you?

The successful entrepreneur needs to acknowledge and face competition. Notice that we need to focus on both acknowledging and facing competition. Business in America today is full of examples of people who fail to acknowledge competition. In the 1970's the petroleum industry would raise prices unilaterally thinking that people needed gasoline and had no viable alternative to buying gas for their cars. There was no competition in their opinion. Sure they competed with one another but the oil giants did not necessarily recognize the threat of people finding another way to get around without their cars. When supply got short and prices became too high, the petroleum industry saw their monopoly fragmenting. Companies went out of business, merged and consolidated. The failure to acknowledge that people did use their cars less and found alterative transportation resulted in significant damage to the industry.

There are more concrete examples. The neighborhood tavern that opens in the middle of a restaurant district where each restaurant has its own bar and lounge fails to make it after one year. Why? Because if the guy who opened the tavern had acknowledged competition then he would have realized that customers could get their drinks at the restaurants where they were eating rather than go outside to another location. So the tavern fails.

Facing competition is another story. Facing competition means that you develop strategies to make your company distinct. You then use the distinction to attract customers to your business. Your goal is to make them choose you over your competitors. Obviously, you must find distinctions that matter to your customers. If you are selling cars and you offer the only cars with galvanized two tone undercoating you may be distinct. But, if competitors offer cars with stainless steel undercarriages then customers are not likely to appreciate how your cars are distinct. But, if your car gets 25% better gas mileage than any of your competitors that is a distinction that probably matters to customers. Hopefully, you will be savvy enough to realize that the gas mileage advantage rather than the two tone galvanized undercoating was the difference customers appreciated.

Facing competition does not mean that you are doing anything to your competitors. It means that you are doing things for your business so that it competes. Ripping on competitors, mud slinging, smear campaigns and attacks on your competition are suited to the dignified world of politics but have no real place in business. I have to hand it to politicians for having the insight to recognize the deeply held belief by the electorate that anyone who runs for public office is a pretty terrible person and that your only choice is the lesser of two evils. Thereby, by pointing out how the other candidate is a more terrible person than they are, they provide the voters with a basis to make their decision. "Well, this guy is a rolling heap of crap but, I saw his commercial and as he so aptly pointed out, the other guy is an even bigger tool. So I will vote for this guy because he is not as bad as the other guy." For future reference, the next time you think about anyone in politics realize that the person elected was merely thought to be less of a pile of crap than the alternative. You know how government would get better? If all politicians realized that they were merely the lesser piece of crap than the guy that they beat. If a person's only qualification for a job is that he or she was the best pile from a steaming heap than the job is not in good hands. But if politicians recognized this about themselves maybe, just maybe, some would be inspired to strive to be better. Hopefully they will recognize that it is not that high a standard. All they need to do is be a slightly less pile of crap. Think about that campaign slogan. "Vote for me because although I know that I am only slightly less offensive than the other candidate, I will try to be a little less crappy than I really am." That guy would get my vote of for no other reason than his candor. Hey, what do you know, "candor" and "candidate" start the same way. It seems odd that the words are so different. But, I digress . . .

My point is that you are not competing like a politician. You have self respect. You want what you offer for sale to be the best it can be not merely a better pile of crap than that of your competition. Facing competition means that you appreciate that your customers may have alternatives and that you need to set yourself apart. Facing competition means that you realize that your competitors set the bar as to what customers expect. You also want to set the bar higher. An industry with healthy competition keeps seeing the bar being raised. This benefits customers. If you face your competition, it also benefits you. It pushes you. It makes you strive to be better. If you do not, you get beat.

People in business for themselves do not relish getting beat by the competition. For that reason, they are ever mindful that they have to strive to do better everyday. There is almost an innate paranoia about what their competitors are doing that causes them to push themselves. This type of paranoia is healthy in disciplining entrepreneurs to keep pushing themselves. Some will be driven by a desire to always win. Nothing less will satisfy them. Losing will not be accepted. These individuals tend to be highly focused, effective and successful entrepreneurs. They are also the truest competitors.

I recall a story relayed to me several years ago by a man who had a son who ran marathons. The father had an interest in how his son was doing in his chosen sport and he recognized his son's deep passion for running and for competing in marathons. One day, the father came home from work and being aware that his son had run a marathon that day, the father asked his son how he did. The son responded simply, "I didn't win." The father recognized the son's disappointment and risked a follow up question. "Well, how did you finish?" His son retorted, "what's the difference, I didn't win!" The father decided not to push it and offered his son some consolation. Then, as he went to give him a pat on the back, he saw that his son had a second place ribbon in his pocket. "What's this?" The father asked. "You didn't tell me that you came in second." To that, the son replied, "Dad, second doesn't matter, I was trying to win. I didn't win." The father liked what he was hearing and baited his son in objecting, "well second place is pretty respectable." The son looked at his father plainly as if his father did not understand. "My goal was to win. I didn't achieve that goal. What good is respectable?"

This story is the epitome of what makes someone a true competitor. Settling for second is not acceptable. The son in this example is driven. He wants to be the best at the sport he loves. Being the best means coming in first. Successful entrepreneurs have built entire industries on this type of attitude. It is the entrepreneur who wants every customer in their respective industry to want their products or services rather than wanting the products and services of their competitors. The best is always distinct from the rest. The best is what everyone should strive to be. And once you are the best, you should fight to make sure that you do not get knocked off that perch. Let your competitors make you better. Let them challenge you to become the best themselves.

Regrettably, however, people who are driven to be the best are often thought to be assholes. Everyone has seen people like this and we have all slipped into that community of thought that, because they are so driven. We condemn them as being heartless, aggressive psychos who have to win at all costs. We relate to others who also condemn them. Collectively, we resent them for pushing themselves and being better than us. The next time you see someone who really pushes himself or herself to succeed and you and other people disparage him or her, take a whiff. Do you know what you will smell? Jealousy. You will be lousy with it and so will the other people agreeing with you. We condemn those people who can commit and make sacrifices to be the best. We denigrate them not because we are jealous of what they have achieved. We are jealous of their fortitude to perform and to achieve their goals. The more lofty their goals and the more that they achieve them, the more we despair at how high they set the bar for all the rest of us.

In so many cases, the jealousy leads people to seek the Achilles heel of these individuals. It seems that the rest of the world is not satisfied until we prove that the person who has more self discipline than anyone else is not perfect. The media is obsessed to always find the weakness of people. Only occasionally do we celebrate the ones with the hardest work ethic and the determination to compete. In sports, we do recognize these individuals and we hail their accomplishments but we are always happy to hear about their human frailty as well. "Oh sure the guy is an all star but he has fathered so many children to unwed mothers he is the defendant in a class action paternity suit." Maybe this makes us feel better about not possessing the gumption that these individuals have. It is sad really. We cannot have immortal heroes. They must have some flaw if for no other reason than to make them interesting. The press will not rest until they find out that for all the good that he does, Superman beats his dog.

So there they are. They are the people who are true competitors. They are the ones who are driven. They are the ones who inspire jealousy and resentment from others.   The ones who by their drive and accomplishment make us feel inadequate. We hated these curve breaking bastards in high school and college and we still hate them. Why do they have to be so driven? Damn them!

But, do you know what? The question for you as an entrepreneur should never be "why are they so driven?" The question for you should be: "can I be as driven?" As far as your soul is concerned, if you care about such things, this is a little healthier for you than condemning the self discipline of others. Maybe, by being driven yourself and not focusing on trying to find fault or cracks in the armor of the people who you witness committing to being the best, you can learn to relate to these people. After all, they are successful and you want to be. Maybe, by comparing yourself to them, you can find similarities. Maybe you could exploit the attributes that you share with them to achieve some success for yourself.

All of this sounds good but it depends on you. Do you want to commit to being the best? Do you really want to compete? Do you want to always be looking over your shoulder to see who might be catching up to you? You might as well ask yourself, do you want to have a heartbeat? Competing and pushing yourself and that feeling of satisfaction you get from doing something with true discipline and with the aspiration of being the best is what keeps you interested in the business. It is what being in business is all about. Sometimes, this gets lost in the details but it is worth thinking about every once in a while. You must have this competitive spirit to some extent because many people who do not have the fortitude to open a business of their own have looked at you and said, "what an asshole!" So, it is no great leap for you to relate to that person who wants to be the best. Chances are, you have seen him or her in the mirror.

CHAPTER 16
Do you Feel Appreciated? No? Well of course you Don't

You never feel appreciated in your own business. It is sad. But, it is true. Face it, you never really feel appreciated in anything in life. Do you ever feel that your spouse adores you? Do you ever think that your kids are grateful for everything that you do for them? Do you ever think that they are grateful for anything you do for them? For any of you toying with saying "yeah my kids are grateful for me" ask yourself about the last time you disciplined them. After you punished them for something that they did, did they look at you and say, "you're right. I realize that it was harder for you to punish me than it was for me to be punished and I appreciate you for doing it, I know that you are only trying to teach me right from wrong and I respect you for that, you are trying to make me a better person and I think that's great!" If your kid did not say this then you are not appreciated. If your kid did say all that, then there are many, many parents willing to adopt them.

But I digress. You are not feeling appreciated. Boo hoo. Really I am crying for you. It must be difficult to be so important to the world and not be respected or understood and appreciated for your importance.

Now for those of you who feel that I am being sarcastic, all I can say is: good for you. You seem to be able to understand my attitude towards people being too frail to be entrepreneurs. Face it, if you constantly need gratitude, respect, a pat on the back or any type of recognition from others to feel better about yourself, then you really should rethink your decision to open your own business. Meanwhile, if you are reading this book and you are already in your own business and you need praise from others to feel better about yourself then you have some mental retooling to do. That retooling starts with a firm appreciation on your part for being alone.

Think about being alone. When I say alone, I mean really alone. Think in terms of a deserted island alone. You make fire like Tom Hanks in "Castaway" and you want someone to praise you for it but there is no one there. That is being alone. The world of human experiences are worthless unless those experiences can be shared or related to others. If you have no one with whom to share experiences, then you are alone. A person alone has only his or her self to please. A person alone has only his or her self to encourage and to be encouraged by.

This may not sound all that good but being alone and recognizing that you are alone does not have to be a tragedy. You are alone in your new business. You might have partners or employees or colleagues but at the end of the day, you are still alone. By yourself in this way there is no one there to make you feel good about your success or to castigate you if you fail. If being alone only causes you to feel lonely then you may come to feel that there is no one.

But is there maybe someone who can help you? Yes. He is in the mirror. She stands every where that you do at the exact same time as you. You share the same shadow. The only way to help yourself when you feel alone is by learning to appreciate yourself. I am not saying praise yourself. You need to merely appreciate yourself. You do not have time to praise yourself. I have a theory that your capacity to love others is limited only by your ability to truly love yourself. I would extend that theory to appreciation as well. You can only appreciate others to the same extent that you could absolutely appreciate yourself when you feel or realize that you are alone.

So now, on your own with only yourself to love and appreciate you, you have to realize that you are responsible about how you feel about yourself in your business. As I said before, you do not have time for praise. Frankly, I would further add that you do not have time for criticism either. Criticizing yourself, unless it is constructive, will only undermine your sense of self-worth and your confidence. Therefore if you cannot criticize yourself nor praise yourself, what can you do?

You can assess and analyze yourself as a business person. Do not overanalyze and do not endlessly assess. But, you should assess yourself. How to assess yourself in business would be a book onto itself if the answer were not so simple. To assess oneself in business is to set reasonable goals and determine if you have achieved them within the time frame you set for yourself. In that way, the only thing you can appreciate about yourself is your progress and your success at accomplishing what you have set out to accomplish. You should not praise yourself for this you should merely take notice.

Now what does any of this have to do with your feeling that no one appreciates you? Am I saying that in the absence of anyone else to appreciate you, you should appreciate yourself? Well, frankly, if you cannot appreciate yourself at all then you should see a therapist. In the alternative, if all you do is appreciate yourself to the point where you heap endless praise on yourself, then you should get a book about developing humility. But, if you have enough understanding of yourself to realize that only a minimum amount of limited appreciation for yourself accomplishing your goals is all you should afford yourself and that all other thoughts about appreciation and gratitude are useless in the business context, then you will have no need to feel appreciated by others.

So what about obtaining appreciation and gratitude from others? Well let us look at the other people in the business context who could appreciate you. There are your customers. You would hope that they appreciate you. You want them to be happy that you and your little business exist. You would love it if they were so happy that they called you everyday just to convey their gratitude to the heavens that you were born and that you opened a business that sells to and services them. But oddly enough, customers do not call and do that. They do not have time. And, you do not have time to listen to them. The only way customers can show their appreciation of you and your small business is to buy more from you and pay the bill on time. If not on time, then at their earliest opportunity. If you need more appreciation than that, well then get out of business. Customers and clients are like your kids. They want what they want when they want it and they are not at all interested in showing you their gratitude. Like your kids they do appreciate you but they really do not know it and they certainly cannot come to grips with the compulsion to show appreciation.

But, as I have pointed out, repeat business is a nice way of showing appreciation. From your stand point, it is the only appreciation that you really need and should be the only appreciation that you truly desire. Also, paying their bills on time also shows appreciation. It is required but seldom done without some delay. Therefore, timely paying customers are showing appreciation for you.

What about other people in your business? Can they show

appreciation? Let us look at employees. Can they show appreciation? Employees are even more like your kids than customers and clients. They can never really show appreciation because most are always willing to jump ship for a better offer. Can you blame them? If someone offers more money and less hassles than they face working for you, then why wouldn't they leave you? At least with your kids they have to stay with you. Your kids cannot simply say, "well I think I am going to join the family across the street now because they have a pool and their father never yells at them." (Note to my kids: Say this to me and I will hold the door for you).

Employees work for the pay that they are entitled to and other than some small element of loyalty and obedience to your rules and respect for your business, they really are not required to show you any more appreciation than that. But then again, ask yourself about when you were an employee. When you got your Christmas bonus did you feel that you needed to fawn all over your employer for giving it to you? Did you kiss his or her ass like it was ice cream? Of course not. You thanked them politely but in your mind, you told yourself that you earned it and, whatever they gave you was not enough. The nature of the employee-employer relationship has not evolved enough from the pure master and servant relationships that have existed for centuries such that there is a proper balance of appreciation and gratitude between the two. That is why we have unions and labor boards and "us versus them" mentalities between employers and employees. The relationship is steeped in many years of mutual suspicion and tension.

So what about colleagues? Can they appreciate you? I could write a whole paragraph here but it would be fluff. Unless the appreciation of a colleague can profit you in some way, who cares whether your colleagues appreciate you? Do you appreciate them? That is why when they retire we do not give them a party. We usually give them some sort of roast so that we can take out some last bits of good hearted animosity that we and our other colleagues share towards them. That is why you merely appreciate your colleague when he or she retires but otherwise, who cares.

How about vendors and suppliers? Can they appreciate you? Sure. They appreciate you. Read the very bottom of their invoice. "We appreciate your business." You see, they even told you that they appreciate you. But, unless you have an invoice indicating that they wish for you to pay them, you do not get any written proof of their appreciation. At Christmas time, they may send a card or a fruit basket. That is about the most appreciation you will get. But, not to be a fly in the ointment of holiday good feelings but isn't that fruit basket a bribe for more business. Sometimes those things are guilt inflicters. Is it possible that they are really saying: "Here is a beautiful fruit basket now please buy more stuff from us next year will you. At least buy enough to justify the half a C-note we spent on this stupid fruit basket." In this context, if you need appreciation, that is about all you are really going to get from anyone but yourself. And, even that appreciation has strings attached.

So you are back to the one person who can show you appreciation. That would be you. And as I already said, you do not have time to dwell on how much you appreciate yourself. So the question really becomes, other than a modicum of appreciation for fulfilling the goals you set for yourself, do you really need any appreciation at all? Those of you who have been successfully running your own business for a while knew the answer to that before ever reading this delightfully depressing chapter. Good for you!

CHAPTER 17
My Simple Economic Primer for the Small Business Owner
(Of course, "Simple" is relative)

Why didn't you take economics?   You were an English major. Didn't you not know English by the time you arrived at college. You were an Archaeology major. You even had an Indiana Jones hat. Did you really think that you were going to be digging up bones in Egypt? You took "Phys. Ed. 109-ballroom dancing" and that was a waste of time and tuition. You took "Philosophy 107 -the study of personal feelings" and that was a waste of time and tuition. So why not economics?

Or, for those of you who were more diligent, why did you take economics? Face it, you don't remember a thing from it. Ask yourself, what do you recall from economics. Have you ever applied anything you learned?   Think back about the classes.   I know, you are the girl who remembered that the guy in the last row was really cute. (I took econ so that was probably me).   Or, you are the guy who thought that the teaching assistant was really hot. (Like you had a chance with her-pulease!!!!).

So whether you took economics or not, you probably are all the same. The concepts of economics elude you. Or so you think. In actuality, you apply the basic principles of economics everyday but you do not think about it. Most likely, you apply these principles better because you do not think about them.

But, how do you apply these economic principles without remembering them from school or never having learned them?

The simple answer is not so simple. It is my belief that economics is to some extent instinctive.   You are born with some of these instincts and some are develop in your youth. Generally, by the time you open your own business, you have honed these instincts to the point where you apply economic principles without thought. You just know how to apply these principles.

To define economics, here is the only formula you need to remember:

infinite needs and wants = finite resources

This formula defines economics. It defines all economics. It is at the heart of every fundamental course of study concerning economics. It is economics.

Home economics, or "Home Ec'" as you referred to it in high school, is the study of how individual consumer units, such as families, acquire, distribute and utilize resources. Typically, the underlying concept in Home Ec' is trying to make the most of fixed streams of income. Then, using principles concerning expense analysis, the typical home economist determines the best way to allocate resources for long term and short term planning (i.e. savings and shopping).

Micro Economics is the study of the application of economic principles to an individual business unit. Your small business enterprise and the study of how it allocates and utilizes resources is micro economics. The underlying concepts studied in micro economics is analysis of fixed and variable costs, supply and demand models and strategies for maximizing profit over fixed and variable costs.

Macro economics is the study of entire industries and national and world economies. The underlying concept is how resources are managed nationally and globally as well as how industries operate in the context of national and international economies.

So why is any of this important to you? You are right. It is not. Go to the next chapter. You did not need to learn economics in high school or college and you do not need to learn it now. You have an archeology degree for goodness sakes. You can apply enough of that to understand economics and what it means for your small business. Or you have an English degree. You can apply enough of what you know about grammar and literature to solve the economic issues you will undoubtedly encounter in your business. Or, you have a business degree in marketing or accounting and they made you take one micro and one macro economics course and you learned all this stuff although you never learned how to apply what you learned in any practical situations. Well then, this chapter is of no use to you. You are right and you are going to be fine. Why did I even write this Chapter?

But, if you are still reading, think about what that business degree person from the last chapter said. She said that she learned all the concepts in her economics classes but she never learned anything about the practical applications of the concepts. For those of you who did not take economics, I already told you the only formula that you really need in order to understand the rest of this chapter. This chapter will be about practical applications of that economic principle. Did you forget it? Here it is again.

infinite needs and wants = finite resources

Here is the practical way of saying it so that it means something to you. You have your business. You need everything, you want everything. You cannot have everything. That is it. The whole shabang. There is nothing tricky or complicated about that is there?

Well now you want to know how this formula works. How could it contain an equal sign between two things that are not equal? The word infinite appears on one side and the work finite appears on the other. How do you make these equal?

Making them equal is what you do as a personal economist everyday. You balance your needs and wants with what you can acquire and possess. You are an economist to your business as well. You take what you have in your business and maximize what you can get from it and for it in order to fulfill what you need and want in your business. You are what balances the equation. You are pitted between infinite wants and needs and finite resources. You are the equal sign!

So now you wonder, how do I make them equal? You do it so many times without thinking about it that it might be difficult to recognize. You cannot see oxygen but so long as you are breathing you know that it is there. Your ability to strike economic balances is there but because it comes so naturally, you do not always realize it.

Think about your business. Do you have every piece of the most expensive office equipment in the world or do you have what you can afford? Are you letting your drivers make deliveries in brand new Mercedes sedans or eight year old Chevy S-10 pickups? They would probably like the Mercedes better. You would probably like the Mercedes better. But, despite your want for that, you have them drive what you can afford. You put things on the balance. You do not need to have your drivers makes deliveries in brand new sedans. You only need for them to make deliveries in a car that is safe and reasonably reliable. But still you want that Mercedes. Of course you do. It represents your unlimited wants. But because the amount of money you can spend on delivery transportation is finite, you spend the least necessary to fulfill your needs. Good job, equal sign.

The heart of understanding the economics of your small business comes down to you being the determining factor of what needs and wants get addressed and how. You then make the distribution determination. You accept the fact that some wants, and quite possibly some needs, go unsatisfied. You cannot do anything about that because you are trying to satisfy those needs with limited resources. You can only apportion what you have. Your needs and wants will always be unlimited.

Now that you understand your function in the formula, you need to work on how to be a better distributor of the limited resources to the unlimited needs and wants. Some people feel that needs only should be addressed first before you even consider mere wants. This makes sense until we tweak the definitions of needs and wants. You might want a vacation but do you need one? If you have been working to the point where your productivity is suffering and you cannot refocus and recharge your batteries then a vacation may be a need. You might want a new laptop but do you need one. If the one you are using is running DOS as its operating system, that new laptop might be more of a need than a want. But if it is a need, do you need the most expensive one with WIFI and all the bells and whistles or one that is so sophisticated that Bill Gates would be jealous? Playing games with the definitions of needs and wants can distort the way in which you distribute the limited resources at your disposal.

"At your disposal" is an important concept. To say that something is at your disposal means that you determine what happens to it. You decide if you need it and if you do, you decide how you will use it. A business may have a credit line at its disposal. If it does, then the owner decides whether he will use the money for expensive lunches or office supplies. At your disposal implies that you have control over your limited resources.

The word disposal should trigger some thoughts for you. A disposal is a place where we discard refuse. To have an asset at your disposal means that you can decide to discard them. Why would you ever discard one of your limited resources? Well, if you have used the resource completely then you might want to discard it as you would garbage. If you have gotten twenty years out of your pickup truck and it is always in the shop and costing you more money to fix than to replace it, you might need to discard it because it is no longer a viable resource but is instead something adding to your needs and wants. Old assets that cannot produce resources for you tend to move from one side of the equation to the other. This causes a strain on your ability to balance as the needs and wants side of the equation becomes heavier while the resources side simultaneously becomes lighter.

The practical application of the formula requires that you, as the owner of the business, make decisions based upon the formula. So for purposes of decision making, you have to consistently inventory the right side of the equation. You must always know what your resources are and you must be realistic as to how and when you can use them. You must also know when it is time to prioritize any particular need or want.

For example, if one of your resources is your accounts receivable then you need to know approximately how quickly you collect in order to know when you can use the cash from your receivables. Your receivables might not be collectable for thirty days. Therefore, in deciding when to spend cash on any particular need or want of the business, you need to schedule the satisfaction of that need or want for thirty days or more. If your fax machine breaks down and it is essential to your business, you probably have to prioritize that need. Therefore, you might need to pull resources from other needs in order to rectify the emergency and buy a new fax machine.

Now here is another tricky part. The factors in the formula are dynamic and not static. Your needs change. Your wants change. Your resources change and sometimes are dissipated or depreciate. You need to continue to maintain the balance despite the fact that the factors on both sides of the equations change over time. For that reason, as a good economist you need to constantly analyze the factors on both sides of the equation. You need to note how the factors are changing. You need to determine how to adjust in order to reestablish the balance.

This might be difficult. It might be impossible. When it becomes impossible, it is time to close shop. If your resources cannot in any way ever satisfy the minimum necessary needs of the business, then the business cannot go on. However, if the balance can be reestablished by some action on your part, then you can save the business. It might require your creativity in using resources. If you can use your delivery truck to transport products for other companies who need deliveries in the same areas as you are already delivering to your customers, then maybe you can go into the delivery business on the side. This adds to the value of resources. Or, adjusting the balance might require your discipline in restraining some of your needs and wants. You might have to say, "sorry but we cannot rent a bigger office because our current cash flow, as a resource, is too small to pay a higher rent." This dispenses with a need or want as a result of understanding your limited resources to afford the need or want. Maybe, adjusting the balance will require using both your creativity in using resources and addressing a need or want. For example, if you need a bigger space for your office and you could find a larger space that costs less per square foot than what you are paying now and you could sublet a portion of the new space, then you might utilize a new resource while simultaneously addressing a need.

In understanding the economics of your small business in this context, you can begin to appreciate that you are what makes the business economically efficient and/or feasible. Assessing resources means that you take them for more than their face value and you are forever interested in finding ways to make the most of those resources. In analyzing your needs and wants you are forever prioritizing and defining those factors in order to satisfy them appropriately. Most importantly, by applying yourself to the basic economic formula of infinite needs and wants equaling finite resources, you are resolving economic issues everyday as a natural part of being an entrepreneur. Even you animal husbandry majors can do this.

CHAPTER 18
Profits and Prophets

Anyone who is a creature in a capitalistic environment craves two intertwined abilities. They want the ability to maintain and maximize profits and they want to profitably forecast the future. Basically, you want to be profitable and prophetic. If you can accurately predict the future, then you can make a profit on all the decisions you make that involve risk. The profitability of any enterprise is directly linked to management's ability to be prophetic. You have to have some capacity to accurately predict what decisions will result in what types of gains and which ones could result in losses. Knowing, based on accurate forecasting, when to commit to certain decisions in search of profitability is the very essence of management of your own business. But what can you do to be a better prophet in order to be more profitable? First, you need to focus on what is profit and then focus on what anyone needs to be more prophetic.

The decisions you make will necessarily involve making decisions that ultimately must result in profits. In thinking about profits, however, you should not always focus on the bottom line. Profits and the bottom line, although similar, are not the same. Bottom line thinkers sometimes get too caught up in capping costs and in doing that they fail to take risks that ultimately prove to be very profitable. If you are in business then you should take risks. This helps everyone. Someone risked the start up costs to create the cellular phone that in the past 20 years have gone from a few "brick" phones in the briefcases of top executives all the way to millions of itty-bitty flip phones in the jean pockets of high school kids.

So, if you do not focus on bottom line and costs, what should you focus on? Focus instead on maximum and minimum profit from any particular decision. Determine what is the most that you could make on any particular decision. Determine also what is the worst potential result of that decision. For example, let us imagine that you have an opportunity to purchase, at a severely discounted rate, an oversupply of something that you either sell or incorporate into one of your products. You determine that the per unit cost savings to you would increase your per unit profits by 20%. If you sold all of the units necessary to deplete the oversupplied item to zero, you would maximize your profits at 20% higher than normal. Now, you also need to look at the worst case scenario, if the oversupply is a perishable item, can you sell any of it in time to avoid the expiration date? If not, that could result in a huge loss. Now ask about other scenarios. Do I suffer a loss if I use the credit line in order to make the purchase? If so, that cuts into that 20% increased profit in a perfect scenario.

After factoring in all the potential best and worst cases then you can start being a prophet. First, without obsessing about the worst that can happen, acknowledge that any decision can have bad results for reasons totally beyond your control. Determine what things can happen that would result in the worst case scenario. Then assess the likelihood of any of those things happening. Finally, determine what can be done to avoid, or to whatever extent, to diminish the likelihood of those things happening.

For example, if you bought the oversupply of items that are perishable, try to assess whether the market is strong enough to sell all that you bought. If the market has been on a down turn, well you need to consider that. All of this seems obvious right? Well, yes and no. Sometimes in business for ourselves decision making has to happen so quickly that we do not do proper assessments. This is only one of the two problems with decision makers these days.

There are two components to decision making. The first component requires thinking. Assessing is yet another word for thinking. Contemplating is also a good word. Analyzing is a terrific word. All of these words convey what the first component of decision making is. It is the thought process that comes before you make the decision. Many people fail to do that. They do not think before deciding. The problem is that all of their decisions will require blind luck in order to achieve success.

The other component seems simple enough. You have to decide. Some think for so long that they never make the decision. There is another chapter in this book that deals with this problem. For our purposes now, just recognize that once you have thought about a decision, you need to close the transaction and actually make the choice. The best way to think about the two components is: plan and execution. You think about the decision and you plan. Then you execute when you decide.

Now before completing the thought process involved in your decision making, you need to rely upon your abilities as a prophet. In order to be more prophetic you need to imagine how you can maximize the profit of your given decision. You need to picture it in your mind. If you cannot at least imagine being successful, then you most likely cannot be successful. Note however, actually succeeding requires work and not merely dwelling on day dreams about being successful. So all you need to do is picture in your mind what the successful result will be. Now imagine, or picture, what happened immediately before the eventual success. Then extrapolate backwards each step toward that success and imagine each step. Commit to that series of pictures and make it happen.

Please do not confuse this with mere positive thinking. Decision making in the business context cannot be managed by the good feeling "think positive" approach that helps people through their addictions etc. This is different.

In our approach, you are merely visualizing, in your head, what the successful result feels like and what steps lead to that success. The steps toward success might not all be pretty pictures. This is a departure from positive thinking. The steps toward success, as you visualize them, may morph into pictures of hard work, extraordinary effort and long nights. That may be a distraction that blurs the image in your head of the ultimate success. But, the steps are necessary to get to your success. In this way, your thinking has to change in order to be more prophetic. You must recognize that success is not a single photograph but is instead the final few frames of a movie that usually depicts adversity and challenges that have been overcome. If you are going to picture your success then you have to visualize the road to it. That road may entail hardships necessary to achieve success. You will need to picture those hardships while also remaining able to picture your ultimate success.

As you begin to develop your imagination in this way, you will be amazed at how quickly you develop the ability to accurately begin to forecast future events. Experience will play a role but the method will help in developing that experience. As you begin to develop confidence in making accurate predictions, you will know, or at least have a better idea, what decisions will be more profitable than others. Over time, your thought process will include an assessment of worst and best case scenarios, determinations as to what to avoid and visualization of not only the ultimate success of your enterprise but the way you arrived at it.

PART III
Casts, Characters and Role Playing in the Business Environment

CHAPTER 19
Mom v. Pop Businesses

We hear the phrase "a Mom and Pop business" all the time. Think about what it means. Typically, a "Mom and Pop" business implies a small company run by two people who are married to each other. This form of business enterprise is indicative of the numerous family businesses that were the backbone of the United States' economy throughout much of the twentieth century. We all know of one or more of these family businesses. Many of them are restaurants or hardware stores or small grocers or construction companies or adult bookstores or professional sport teams or funeral homes or motorcycle dealerships or computer software design firms. In truth, there are "Mom and Pop" businesses in almost every type of industry. It has become a very common business form. For that reason, we need to delve beyond the cliché and study this type of business not only for those readers who are in "Mom and Pop" businesses but for those readers who can learn from them.

Think about the dynamic of two people running a business that is the livelihood of both of them and is usually the sole source of income for their entire household. Add to this, the owners and operators of that business being in a committed romantic and/or emotional relationship. How do they balance the pressure of marriage and the pressure of operating a business together? As you think about it, imagine all the situations that are vulnerable to the operators manipulating one another. You can hear a wife say, "we will have my parents over for Thanksgiving and then the company can afford to send you on that business trip." Imagine all the situations and all the emotional blackmail that goes on in these types of businesses. "You will get some this weekend if I can get a new company car. Okay?" Imagine how the line between the business interest and the marriage becomes blurred in these businesses.

In my experience, calling these businesses "Mom and Pop" companies is not accurate. "Mom versus Pop" is more accurate. Once there is an emotional bond amongst the people operating the business, there is an increased frequency and intensity of conflict. Marital issues come into the business and the business is a major source of marital issues.

What is the real reason for the conflict? Here is a clue: it is the root of all evil. You guessed it. It is money. Money and financial issues for any business are difficult to jibe amongst two or more owners. But, when the two owners must make almost perfect financial decisions or risk the ability to sustain themselves, then that magnifies the conflicts that result from financial decisions.

Do you want an example? Think about a "Mom versus Pop" company facing a decision to expand the business by spending more or deciding to put the money aside for the owners' retirement. It is a daunting task just thinking about the arguments that would come up in light of the competing interests of preserving marital harmony and risking losing business opportunities that present themselves. The worst part of this is that you can think of justifications for both sides of the argument. Either choice has merit. The difference is that one benefits the marriage and one benefits the business. Take this one to a mediator and he or she will excuse himself or herself half way through the mediation to go into another office to cry. This is a problem without a perfect solution. What is worse is that one party has to win and one has to lose. That might not have a significant effect on the business relationship but might be detrimental to the marital relationship. Whenever one spouse wins an argument, the other has to suffer the indignity of losing. The winner then has to suffer the possibility that they forced the issues, beat their spouse and then the decision turns out to be wrong. We all know what comes next. "I told you so!"

Then, just to make things more complicated, the business becomes the couple's major form of socializing. Many or all the friends of the couple are from business relationships. If Mom and Pop break up who gets the business and who gets the business contacts? What happens when the married couple has no outside interest other than the business and then the business does not live up to their expectations?

106

All of these thoughts can bring you pretty far from the simple concept of a "Mom and Pop" business that you might have had when you started reading this chapter. They are complicated. As you think about all the complications of what you took for granted as being pretty straightforward, it makes you wonder why people get married. It makes you wonder why people open their own businesses. And then you wonder about any married coupled opening their own "Mom versus Pop" business . . . Jesus!

Yet, for all of its complexities, it is one of the most enduring business structures in the world of commerce. The answer as to why it is so popular is as complicated as the study of the business form itself. In order to begin to understand why, however, is to recognize that there is a special dynamic in the "Mom versus Pop" business that makes it effective for operating many small businesses. It is hard to describe or quantify that dynamic, but it is there. I have several theories about that dynamic nonetheless.

One theory is that the mutual trust amongst married people helps them to more effectively deal with certain business issues. For example, employees can be treated more like children and therefore they can be more effectively managed. Also, some business situations naturally lend themselves to an "us versus them" mentality. A married couple can bring themselves together to tackle problems such as unfair competition or slow payers or unruly suppliers. The solidarity between the married operators of the business in dealing with outside forces prohibits the outside forces from playing one owner against the other. A house, or a business, not divided against itself seems to stand up pretty well to outside threats.

Another theory about why "Mom v. Pop" businesses are sometimes more enduring than other businesses is that some married people compete with their other spouse to some extent. In the context of this being a healthy competition, it can benefit the business. He goes out of his way to bring in more business. She does not want to deal with his ego so she finds a way to make the business that they already have more profitable. So long as they do not allow the competition to permeate to the point that they try to undermine each other, there is a benefit. So if she is bringing in new business, it would not be good for him to push that same business away because he does not want to acknowledge her success. Nevertheless, when

107

both the Mom and Pop are driven, even if that drive is the result of competition with one another, the business could be the winner.

Another theory as to why some Mom v. Pop businesses have an advantage is that marriage often by its nature causes a delegation of certain duties and eliminates overlapping and doubling of efforts for certain tasks. When a married couple carries this over into the business, it provides for greater efficiency. Think about how many businesses you see where two owners do exactly the same thing. Duplicity of their efforts on one thing usually results in other things not getting done. But, married couples who are used to having delegated different tasks to one another in maintaining a household can usually do the same in operating the business. She handles the books and he handles the sales desk. She works with the customers and he works with the suppliers. She handles payroll and he handles the employees. Much of this is a carry over from the typical delegation of tasks that takes place in the marriage. She handles the bills and he cuts the lawn. She does the laundry and he purchases the groceries. He goes to the kids' soccer games and she decorates the living room.

There are numerous other theories or reasons why the marital relationship can benefit a business. The important thing to recognize for any business owner who is in a family business or is not, is that it is possible to imitate some of the things that make family businesses more dynamic and successful. It is also important to recognize those things that make the family businesses susceptible to greater pressure for their owners and operators.

Any business owner should realize that a total mutual reliance and/or dependence upon the business as the sole income to their respective households raises the stakes in decision-making. Owners should be conscious of one another's feelings, thoughts and most of all needs. Owners of any business should appreciate that the relationship enjoyed amongst the owners outside of the business relationship needs definition and consideration just the same as it does for married couples running a business. Owners should have friends outside of the business and outside of one another's social circle. Conflicts involving the business should be related to the business only and not subject to manipulation by the individual operators for matters outside of their business relationship.

Business owners and operators should also recognize, however, that it is good to have healthy competition amongst the operators of the business. They should strive to delegate tasks and authority much the same way a married couple does. They should develop a relationship with their fellow operators and owners that demonstrates unity to those who would seek to fracture that relationship and by doing so hurt the business.

Finally, the one other element that one experiences in dealing with a family business is completely abstract but nevertheless undeniably present. Dealing with a family business has a certain feel. It is almost impossible to define but you know it when you feel it. Family businesses give off an aura that perhaps no other business can mimic in the exact same way. You get a sense that you, as a customer, are more important to the members of a family business. You feel that more than one person is interested in your satisfaction as a customer. You sense that you are dealing with a team more than merely an individual salesperson. Much of this good feeling can be attributed to dealing with a small business but there is something about being a customer of a family business that makes you feel good. As indescribable as it is, it is a feeling that all business owners should strive to make their customers feel. It is the type of feeling that brings customers back, time and time again.

CHAPTER 20
"_____(your business name here) The Next Generation"
Look Out For Junior

Maybe you have seen Star Trek. Some of us can remember it when it was on network television from 1966 to 1968 as opposed to Sunday morning syndication for many years after that. (Hey Trekkers, was Yeoman Rand the hottest Star Trek Babe of all time or what? See you at the convention? Psych, I won't be there as I am busy writing books and running a business and being married and raising children although I wish that I could go). Anyway, if you are familiar with the show you might recall that it was reinvented about 20 years after the original was cancelled and brought back as "Star Trek, The Next Generation." If only your business had the staying power of the entire Star Trek concept. More than forty years after its original debut, it still has nearly rabid followers.

What has this got to do with your business? Well "Star Trek" and "Star Trek, the Next Generation" can teach you something about the continuation of your business beyond your limited life and productive employment span. What happens to your business when you are ready to retire? Have you thought about that? With you no longer at the helm, who is going to steer your enterprise? (Those familiar with the show will recognize the play on words). What will the next generation of your business be like?

The first thing you need to wrap your mind around is the idea that it will not be exactly the way you ran it. Time changes things. New technologies, philosophies and economies will come and go and your business will need to adapt and change in order to survive. There is a saying that people never change. That may be true. People have a limited life span and in the relatively short amount of time anyone inhabits the earth, there is little or no reason to change. My theory about typical human longevity is that we humans live relatively short lives of, on average, less than a full century because of our limited ability to adapt. But, we are living longer than our predecessors as a result of our individual increasing ability to adapt. Our minds are not closing as fast as those of our predecessors.

But just as we humans have limited longevity, our businesses have unlimited longevity. Look at some of the companies that exist in this world. Many have been around for many generations. Each of these companies has had to pass the reigns onto another generation every twenty years or so in order to continue to exist and prosper. They do so because these businesses are dynamic. They can, and recognize that they must, adapt and change. The Union Pacific Railroad, Wells Fargo and Western Union are not operating as they did back in the 1800's. They have transformed into different types of companies over the years. The people who started those companies have handed control to others who have done the same time and time again. Each new crop of operators has lived in a different time and a different business reality. They have been the driving force of their respective companies' ability to adapt and change.

I personally do not believe that anachronism can survive in today's business climate. You cannot run a business with antiquated ideas. I would go so far as to say that you cannot run a business without fresh ideas. The people running a business must commit to a vision of the business operating in a certain time and within the context of a certain business reality. For example, in the past, people took for granted that other people would pay their bills. It was a source of embarrassment if a company or person could not pay their bills on time. In that business climate, companies could operate under the understanding that the overwhelming majority of people and companies would pay on time. There were significantly more cash transactions. Rarely did a company fail to pay. Today, things are different. Companies and people take special pride in being able to pay on time. The majority of companies do not pay on time and there appears to be little shame in that. A significant amount of transactions today are done on credit. Cash deals are not very plentiful as opposed to in the past when cash deals were the norm. Based on this analysis, anyone operating a business today who fails to research the ability of its customers to pay their bills is living in the past. As such, they are an anachronism operating in peril of facing serious cash problems. You cannot trust people to pay as well as they did in the past. If you operate under this belief, you do so at a significant risk.

So as you think about your business, are you now or will you be prepared to hand it over to the next generation when the time comes? What can you expect and how can you plan for that exchange?

The first thing you must recognize is that just the same way that the original "Star Trek" was different from "Star Trek, the Next Generation" your business will be different in the hands of the people who run it after you. The people will be different and the time in which they are running it will be different. The people after you will have the benefit of greater education and more fluid flows of up to the minute information. They will operate the business in a new age of different state and federal regulations. They will operate in the wake of new technologies. They will operate in a climate that has many industries that are different from the ones we know today.

A generation ago, there was no internet. All but the largest, wealthiest and most advanced companies had no computers much less networks. There were no cell phones but there were these things we called telephone booths. (Try to find a pay phone today. They used to be in every public place and on many busy streets). In those days, an Etch-a-Sketch was a laptop marvel rather than an IBM Thinkpad. Many of the cash registers did not require an electrical outlet. Credit cards were not used to buy fast food. Fast food consisted of little more than hamburgers, hot dogs and later tacos. In those days, you could board a commercial plane in less than fifteen minutes from your car to your seat. People operating businesses a generation ago faced different situations as a result of what was available and what was normal at that time.

Think about the businesses that existed back then and still exist today. I had an IBM Selectric typewriter back then. It was as big as my current photocopier and it weighed about as much as my SUV. Now, I doubt that IBM produces any seven products that have a combined weight of one Selectric typewriter. IBM changed and adapted. New people are in place there who have responded to new inventions. We do not even have to get into where products are manufactured today as opposed to where my old Selectric was made. (One thing to be thankful for as manufacturing has moved out of the United States is that we all have a better understanding of world geography. I had never heard of a place called Sri Lanka when I was in school but now I know that it is where my shirt was made). It is amazing how things change.

So you have to accept the idea that in the next generation, things will change. Maybe they will be better but it is unlikely that those of us operating a business now will see it that way. Our successors will probably think of how primitive we were in running our business in the time period we ran it. The next generation will marvel at how we needed a keyboard as an input device on our computers. "You mean they didn't have telepathic integration with the internet back then? How did they ever make references to things as they communicated with one another?" Or, "they carried this script called cash? What a waste of trees. How did they ever get the cash into the fingerprint scanners in order to buy things? Then they had to keep receipts in order to 'file' tax returns? Are you kidding me? How is it the government did not know about every transaction as it does now?" Or, "you mean that they used to buy things over the internet and have it shipped to them? It took how many days? Why didn't they use an instant holographic teleporter or a 3-D fax?" If that is what they will think of us then so be it. Things will be different in the future and businesses will adapt.

When thinking about all of this you need to appreciate the legacy that your business is and what that represents to you. Perhaps there are fundamental principles that you always want to be the cornerstone of your business. Perhaps you always want it to be committed to excellent service or integrity. These are good things to want and they are good things to try to preserve as your business goes forward without you. You can never be sure that these principles will endure in your business but you can increase the likelihood that they will. The best way to do that is to be particular about who the next generation of operators of your business will be.

Captain Kirk did things his way. Captain Picard did things his way. But, despite being 90 years apart in time, there were common characteristic of both individuals. Both were courageous and moral and although they captained two very different Enterprises, they both were committed to the same goals as they explored space.

In your business, you can find people who are willing to move the business forward who share the same dedication to your guiding principles. Provided that your principles are general enough to transcend time, then you can find people who can observe those principles and take over for you. Then equipped with your personal legacy to the business and the education and appreciation for the business climate in which they will be working, there is no reason to believe that your business cannot proceed and prosper in the next generation.

Where to Find a Successor?

In looking for these wonderful people who will be Jean Luc Picard to your Captain Kirk, maybe, just maybe, your search should start in your own backyard. As humans, we have the God given ability to manufacture other human beings. This was a major commercial undertaking when commerce in the United States principally consisted of farming. It took man power to operate the farm so farmers, with the help of their spouses, manufactured homemade laborers to work the farm. Kids were not merely used for welfare and tax deductions back then. The intention was to have kids so that they could work. When the kids grew up, they would inherit the farm. They were trained from birth to be farmers. I can only imagine how many of my clients would be happy to hear that in the old days, people had kids who were expected to help support the family as opposed to being the ones who needed to be legally supported to the tune of 20-30% of one spouse's gross income. "You mean to tell me that kids were once useful?" And I answer, "yeah, in the old days they were." Sometimes the old days had certain advantages.

Like anything else, there are pros and cons to handing operation of your business over to junior. There is a nature and nurture debate that could fill an entire other book. Is Junior the product of your genes or is he or she made up of experiences in an environment that you are not connected to? If you worked for everything you ever got and started humbly in a hovel, can Junior really appreciate enough about being hungry from you merely telling him or her what it was like? Does Junior respect you enough to operate the business with the same principles you espoused?

There is a family dynamic to having your children come into the business much like the dynamic between a husband and wife in a Mom v. Pop business. Of course, there are elements that are very different as well. Being in the same family adds an ingredient to the employer-employee relationship that you might not have counted on. I can yell at my kids differently and more forcefully and with significantly more abuse than I might use on someone else's kid. That is one of the few benefits of parenthood. But in dealing with your own kids differently than you do other people's kids who are working for you, do you assess them the same way? Do you assess them fairly? Are your expectations higher of your own kids because you think that they should either be more loyal to you or more like you? Should they have greater motivation because they are your kids? Or, do they see through what others who have not lived with you for their entire lives cannot? Can your kids recognize your weaknesses more quickly and therefore manipulate you or situations to suit them? Are you likely to succumb to the little bastards who will eventually be choosing your nursing home?

There is no set formula in being able to assess the value of having your own kids come into the family business and eventually take over. There are merely things to consider. If you want exact answers, you are going to have to pay a lot more than the cover price of this book. More importantly, if you think that there are exact answers, you are fooling yourself.

So if all you can do is consider things, then you should assess your kids as potential successors as you would any other candidates. Because you probably cannot be objective, go outside of yourself to perform the assessment. Have customers meet Junior. Ask them to be candid in giving you and assessment. Make sure that they know why you are asking and make them comfortable that they will not hurt your feelings. They probably will withhold any criticism that would hurt your feelings no matter how much you assure them that they will not, but, you should still listen to what they say. If they offer no opinion other than a polite, "yeah, he will do fine" without enthusiasm, then you should consider that a comment. If you can extrapolate from that that the customer would leave if Junior took over, then you should consider that as well. You do not want to leave a business to Junior that is destined to fail because he or she is abrasive. Remember, that business is your kid also. You have a responsibility not to marry the business off to someone who will not take care of it.

Outside of customers, have suppliers, colleagues and other business acquaintances meet Junior. If competitors are strong supporters of Junior's candidacy, well then consider the source. Think about what that support says. Read between the lines to see that by your competitor's endorsement, they are saying "yes, by all means, have Junior take over as we see a future advantage for ourselves because your kid is an idiot." If your kids get along with the people you do business with, then that should go a long way to demonstrating the strength of their candidacy.

Finally, ask employees. They are so often overlooked in these situations. A guy operates the business for years and builds up a staff of twenty people who have been with the company for years and years. Then, he brings in Junior and before he knows it, all the employees start to quit and move on. Coincidence? Maybe, if you are willing to believe in that level of coincidence. If you can get past believing in that level of coincidence however then you ask yourself, "I wonder if they do not like Junior?" Could that be it?

Now, of course employees do not wish to get fired for ripping on the boss's kid. You can imagine the conversation.

"Hey Joe, what do you think about my kid? Honestly?"

"Well gee Boss, if I can be honest, then I think he's a total butt f - - - loser and I hope the hell you never let him take over because the staff will have a mass exodus if you do and the customers, who somehow have been able to build up an even lesser opinion of Junior than any of us on staff , will leave in droves."

"Really Joe?"

"Well, I could tell you more but I don't want to hurt your feelings Boss."

Now ask yourself how many people you have on staff who are as secure as Joe. I did not think so. So you need to get an assessment from the people who know your business best what they think about Junior but . . . you need to get them to be honest despite the Catch 22.

Try asking for anonymous suggestions. Find some mechanism for having employees tell you what they think about Junior. Then, no matter what they say, do not even get tempted to find out who said what. Think about them. They are the people who if they want to keep working for your business want to see it succeed and prosper. In order to do so, they want you to hand the reigns over to someone who can be successful running it in your stead. This is a good time for you to assess what you know about your staff and you own ability to be objective. Maybe some of your staff want the business for themselves and would love to throw Junior under the bus. Think about all of it.

Finally, ask Junior. Throw out the typical interview questions like, "where do you see yourself in five years? Ten years? Twenty years?" I always loved those questions during an interview because whenever they would ask about twenty years I wanted so much to say, "well hell I have to win the lottery some time within the next twenty years because otherwise I might get stuck working at this place."

Seriously, ask Junior what his or her intentions are. Ask what they would do with the business. Ask what they would do different from you. Ask why they would deserve it. Do not accept an answer such as "because Mom said so." Assess the level of detail in their answers. If there is detail in their answers then that should be an indication that they thought about it. Details come from the imagination. If they have imagined running the business after you are gone, they will have details of what they imagined. See if they ask you what your plans are. Ask them about various employees and hypothetical situations. Be objective in picturing them in charge based on the answers to the questions. Then, determine if there is any genuine enthusiasm on their part or if they are merely trying to make you happy. Make sure that they know that you support and love them no matter what and that they do not have to go into the family business if they truly want something else. Then, let them know that you have not decided to give it to them so they should not take the business or you for granted.

The most important thing to remember in thinking about keeping the business in the family is to be flexible. Understand for yourself and for your kids that things change. Situations change. Maybe there was a time when they wanted the business but their feelings have changed since then. Maybe they became too complacent and they no longer have the drive to make the business a success. Your own ability to be flexible is the greatest asset you can have in determining whether you should bring the kids into the business and in honestly assessing whether your kids and your business are a good match.

If not Junior, then Who Else should be and When Should you Bring in for the Next Generation?

There really is no set schedule as to when you might bring the next generation of operators on board for your business. There are a number of factors that could affect the decision and timing of the move. The most that anyone could make is suggestions. For example, you should do it before you are completely out of the business. In order for the new operators to learn the business and to appreciate the relationship the business had with you, it is best for them to see you in the business. You should also do it at a time when your company has enough business and cash to bring the person aboard. Also, you should do it early enough before your retirement to properly assess the person but not too early as to have the next generation waiting too long to take over. The examples are potentially endless as there are countless other factors to consider.

Because there are so many factors to consider in determining when it is best to bring the next generation in it could become overwhelming. It is like analyzing a golf swing. There are so many factors that must be done in proper sequence and executed so perfectly that to think about them ruins the swing. Not being able to think about all those things you then rely upon simple "feel." In your golf swing as in any complicated and complex matters that you may face in business, sometimes it is best to stop analyzing and just go with what "feels" right. Otherwise, you may become overwhelmed.

Now there is an upside to bringing the next generation aboard even a little bit early. The business could benefit from having your years of experience and the new education of the youth movement. The combination of those assets could benefit the business greatly. Your experience could help to make certain that you do not make mistakes while the education of the new generation could open up new ways to service customers and more efficient ways to do business. This benefits the new operator as well because they learn from your practical experience while also applying what they have learned in school. Meanwhile, you learn a few things too that maybe they were not teaching from way back when you were in school. I see a win - win situation here, how about you?

Yet another factor to consider, as we touched upon before, has to do with choosing the right person. Sometimes, you happen to meet or employ the absolutely right person to take over after you long before you are ready to retire. There can be no accounting for timing. You might have a particularly good employee who you realize you should bring along and groom to take over for you. You might be a long way from retiring but still

118

you need to bring this person along. In these situation, there are a number of things you can do.

The most important thing to do is ask them what they intend to do. Do they want to stay with the business? Would they be interested in owning it? Maybe, you could transfer small parts of the business to them over time as they continue to work it. For example, if you are planning on retiring in ten years, you could transfer 5% of the ownership per year for the next ten years and then sell the last 50% when you are ready to retire. In this way, you do not lose control until your time and you make it easier for your successor to buy the business. The most important thing in this is to develop mutual recognition between you and your successor of one another's needs and desires. They will want to know that their employment with your business is going somewhere. You want to know that they are worth your time and effort to groom and teach them the business. Because what will be happening to each of you happens over time, you need a commitment to one another.

Much like in good marriages, the best commitments are based on what you can do together in the future as opposed to merely what you meant to each other in the past. If you are grooming a person who you feel loyal to and who has been loyal to the business for years but together you have no plan for the future, you are in danger of making a mistake. Handing over the operation of the business should not be a reward for someone's loyalty. Do not get me wrong, loyalty is valuable but alone, it is not a sufficient reason to turn over the operation of your business to someone who may not be qualified.   There are probably many loyal employees at Microsoft but not all of them can be CEO. (You know that you are successful when your company name "Microsoft" is recognized in the spell check program).

And you also must consider the old brokerage legal disclaimer: "past results are not necessarily indicative of future performance." I love that one. It is like saying, just because the stock has made money in the past you should not count on it making money in the future but we will happily accept your purchase and the commission anyway. The point is that just because an employee you have has been a stellar performer for the business over the years he or she might not be able to continue with that success. Or, they simply might not be cut out for running the show. Not everyone can be a businessaire. Some of them will probably read my other book before taking over the reigns from you and potentially, they may find that running their own business is not for them.

My strongest suggestion is to buy them a copy of this and my previous book and discuss the whole thing after they have read both of them. Do not loan them a copy because I receive no royalties on your desire to share, thank you. But go ahead and buy them my books. I can think of no better way to properly determine if they are capable of running your business than with a firm grasp of the principles of these two fine publications.

As a final suggestion, do not be afraid to be wrong. No one can absolutely predict the future. You may put someone in the business who does a terrible job. So long as you gave some real thought to your decision, do not beat yourself up. You cannot be perfect nor should you expect your successor to be perfect. In this imperfect world the best any of us can do is hope and pray. But then, if you have been a business long enough to think about a successor, you have been doing that already.

CHAPTER 21
"So this Officer for the Company walks into a bar and says to a Shareholder, 'Just what does the board of directors do for the Company?' The Shareholder looks at him and says, "they fire the officers who don't have a clue!"

Directors, officers, partners, shareholders, receivers, trustees, vice-presidents, general managers . . . .the list of roles and positions that people play in businesses today seems endless. Perhaps it is. There are many important jobs that need to be addressed to run a business. Understanding what those jobs are and the duties of the people who assume those jobs is very important to the operation of the business.

Oftentimes, in the context of small businesses, the differences between officers, directors, shareholders and other corporate positions becomes blurred. The reason for that is simple: usually in small businesses one or only a few people hold multiple jobs. As a result, people cannot typically differentiate between when they are being a director, a shareholder, an officer or something else.

The problem with not appreciating the differences is that if other people assume different roles as the business grows the door is open for conflict. If I undertake some action as director and you undertake a different action as an officer for the same company, who has control? As a director, what decisions do I get to make as opposed to you the officer? Does a shareholder get a say? How do we delegate decision making? If these issues cannot be addressed and unless these questions can be answered, the business will not be able to grow. More importantly, if one person has to assume all of these roles in order to preserve harmony, the business will not be able to grow beyond what that one person alone can do. The business will suffer the limitation of having only one person running it.

In this chapter, we will talk about the roles assumed in a basic corporation. In later chapters we will discuss partners and other types of relationships amongst other types of positions in small businesses. For now, however, let us look into the guts of a typical corporation and dissect its parts to determine how it works.

The Hat Trick

Because it is difficult to determine when you are acting as a director, shareholder etc., and because I strive to make the abstract more concrete, I have developed the following exercise. It has many advantages as a teaching method. It is easy. It is comprehensive. It is memorable and it is humiliating. By being humiliating, it forces you to remember so that you do not have to do it again. This in particular makes it effective as a teaching tool. All teaching is humiliating and that is why the humble are more likely to learn.

Sound good? I know, it doesn't but give it a try. Wait until you see what you learn.

We start by taking out three hats. You can use any type of hats that you would like. You can use three baseball caps, painter's caps, visors or just about anything that you can wear on your head. They do not have to be the same type but you might find it more comfortable if each one fits. Next, you need three flash cards or pieces of paper each of which can be attached to each of the three hats.

On one piece of paper, you need to write "Shareholder." On the second please write: "Director." On the third, please write: "Officer." These will be your hat labels. Now some of you already see where I am going but do not jump ahead. Please attach one label to one hat a piece. Now you should have three hats with three different labels identifying a Director, a Shareholder and an Officer.

The best part of this exercise is that you do not need three people. You are going to wear each of the hats. As the business grows, and more people become involved in it, you will be having other people wearing the hats you made. You will also be sharing hats with people. Sometimes you will wear the hat as an officer and you will then share the hat with another officer. The hat that will probably be shared the least is the "Shareholder's" hat if only one or a few people own the business.

For now, we are ready to have you start wearing hats. You have just started your own business. Congratulations! (Sucker!) You have consulted with your attorney and you have filed the necessary paperwork with you state agency that oversees corporations and you now have a new corporation. You own it so you are the first "Shareholder." Put on the shareholder hat. Put it on! I'm not kidding! Put it on! If you do not put it on I will turn this chapter right around and we will not get to Disneyland!!!

See? The hat looks great on you. How are you doing Mr. or Ms. Shareholder? Now that you are a shareholder in a corporation you are the owner. That means you have a right to the profits in this place. Let's see those profits. Well where are they? Oh, you are correct. Unless you do some business, you will have no profits. So let's get the business started.

The business gets started by having the shareholders vote to determine what direction the corporation will go in. With your shareholder hat proudly on your head vote loudly and proudly for your slate of directors for the corporation. Say it with me: I vote for me!

Put on your Director's hat. You could put it on over the Shareholder's hat or you could take off the Shareholder's hat for now. It's your choice.

Now with the Director's hat on, tell yourself, "I accept the shareholders' unanimous nomination and appointment to the board of directors. I will do everything in my power to make the corporation effective and profitable. As a director, I will be responsible to the shareholders and I will strive to be an accurate conduit for conveying corporate information and for advising the shareholders of problems and opportunities to make the corporation grow. I will carry out my fiduciary duties to the corporation and the stockholders to the best of my ability. I will rely upon my experience and education to foster the development, growth and prosperity of the corporation. I thank you for your faith in me."

Now wearing both hats, escort yourself into the other room and assure yourself that the corporation is in good hands. Show the shareholder the door and take off that hat. Now wearing the Director's hat only walk back into the other room and say in a low voice, "My God those shareholders' meetings are a pain in the ass. If I had to spend any more time with that shareholder, I would go nuts. So long as I put a sweet dividend in their pocket at the end of each quarter, they should keep voting me back on the board of directors each year, keep paying my director's fee and leave me alone."

A person on the board of directors for a corporation has a vote in the major decisions affecting the corporation. Usually, as a corporation gets larger, there is one person selected as the "Chairman" of the board. Different corporations handle the chairmanship duties differently but in most cases, the chairman, or chairperson, makes the schedule and agenda. How important is that? Well if the corporation has only a limited amount of funds to devote to certain projects, and the chairperson has certain "pet projects" then the chairperson can put his or her projects on the agenda before other projects. If all the money that the corporation has is used for the first projects discussed at the board of directors' meeting, then the chairperson's pet projects get a priority over other projects that might not get voted on because there is no money left to consider them. The Chairman of the Board wields power by prioritizing what gets discussed by the board of directors. If you have an issue that is not the Chairman's priority, that issue will not get addressed.

Back to our exercise. Still wearing the Director's hat, you walk back into the other room and you realize you better get the business started. You are the Director. You handle the major decision making. You are responsible for the direction of the corporation. But, now you need someone to handle the every day decision making. You need someone to carry out your agenda for moving the corporation forward in your direction. You need rank and file everyday managers and decision makers.

Everyday operations are carried out by officers. So, you decide to carry out your duty as Director and you commence hiring corporate officers. You are a small corporation. You should only need one to get started. You have a resume from yourself on your desk and despite deciphering that a lot of that resume is just fluff and BS, you decide to hire yourself. You negotiate with yourself a salary as corporate officer. You hold out your hand and shake with yourself congratulating yourself on your new job as corporate officer.

Now the everyday stuff begins. You put on your Officer hat and you confirm the direction that the Director has selected for the business. In order to carry out that direction, you need to rent an office for the business. You, as officer, do the research and you find an appropriate space. You negotiate a favorable rent and lease you can live with. You tell the landlord that you will forward the lease to the Directors for ratification. You send it to yourself and then you put on your Director's hat. You review the lease and you make a recommendation to the Shareholder. In your recommendation, you see that the lease needs a personal guarantee. You, as Director, advise the Shareholder that the Shareholder needs to sign the personal guarantee because the fledgling corporation does not have a credit history yet. You put on your Shareholder hat and you sign the personal guarantee. You send the lease back to the Director and you, as the Director, prepare a written corporate resolution adopting and otherwise ratifying the lease. You send the corporate resolution to you as the Officer advising yourself to sign the lease. The Officer signs the lease and gives it to the landlord with a check that the Officer signs from the corporate account for the security deposit and first month's rent. The Officer is now responsible for making sure that the rent gets paid each month so wear that hat when you are writing the rent check.

Wearing your Officer hat you begin ordering supplies and getting the business underway. You deal with the day to day vendors and customers. You conduct the business of the corporation. You make sure that it is running properly. You report to the Director who hired you.

Now, if switching all those hats seemed ridiculous, ask yourself this: do I now understand the difference between what I do as a Shareholder, a Director and an Officer for my corporation? If your answer is "yes" then the exercise was successful. You see, you did all those things before without thinking about it. Now, you are thinking about what you do while wearing which hat. If you commit yourself to always thinking in terms of which hat you wear for each decision you make and each task you undertake, then you can start to think about how you can delegate tasks amongst the major parts of the business. Moreover, if you realize what your duties and obligations are as a Director and Officer and what your rights are, then you can make certain that you do not blur the various roles each serves. You can recognize the importance of executing written resolutions as a Director of the corporation authorizing certain actions. You can recognize that the Director thinks more globally about the corporation while you, as Officer, need to get to the day to day operations. You can appreciate that the Director does not have to decide which supplier to buy from for one particular order.

Now let us say that the corporation grows and you need to spend more time reviewing research from the officers in order to make policy decisions. You need to hire officers other than yourself to carry out your policies for the corporation. With your current understanding of the roles of officers, you can prepare for your officers a specific job description that explicitly outline what decisions they can make without checking with you and what decisions they need to refer to you.

What happens if you are a shareholder and you want to retire or pursue some other line of business or want to open your own business separate from the corporation. As a director, you cannot go into a competing business or just disregard your current obligations to the corporation so you withdraw as director. You only want to be a shareholder. Now you can vote in directors who are answerable to you by virtue of your annual voting. You can select directors who will take the business in a direction to make you money without you needing to be involved in the major decisions or day to day decisions. You can sit back and collect your dividends and pursue whatever other businesses you would like.

Corporations v. Humans, Which would you rather be?

You have all these duties and rights of shareholders, directors and officers. You have your system that dictates who has the power to do what, how and why on behalf of the corporation. You have people exercising authority on behalf of the corporation. The question now becomes, where does the power come from?

The answer: paper. More precisely: paper and ink. The corporation is ruled by its charter or corporate articles and by-laws the same way the United States government derives its authority from the Constitution. The authority of any person on the board of directors to vote on who will be the officers or any other major decisions comes from the corporation's paperwork. The charter, or articles or by-laws in some ways constitute the DNA of the corporation. It is the physical presence of the corporation. It is the only aspect of the existence of the corporation as an individual that is not abstract. Why is it important to think of your corporation in term of its physical books and records? Because, just like some people claim that they can read another person like a book, you really can read your corporation like a book.

In many ways, corporations are like humans. The corporate books provide the proof. The corporation's books contain its memory of all events that have been written down and otherwise documented. A human maintains memories in the recesses of his or her brain. Often times, those memories are unclear or simply completely inaccurate. Corporation's memories are in writing. They cannot be distorted other than by odd interpretation etc. With corporations having a memory that precisely and accurately details in writing what happened, corporations clearly have an advantage over humans when it comes to documenting history.

The corporation's book contains its personality. Unlike humans, the corporation needs written documentation to change its personality. Those changes take place as a result of the people involved in the corporation expressly meeting to discuss the changes and assessing the consequences of the change. Personality changes for the corporation, and its image, needs the blessing of others before those changes can take effect. Meanwhile, humans can change without advanced warning. Humans make personality changes without assessing the potential chaos that can result in instituting the changes. "I do not think that I am cut out to be married anymore, okay Honey?" To which the spouse responds with a bewildered expression, "but what about our three kids and our relationship?" And the first spouse expresses, "those things just are not important to me anymore. You understand don't you?" A human's ability to change personality at the drop of a hat without extensive consultation and approval by a board of directors make humans markedly more volatile than corporation. Advantage: corporations.

The books have the stated purpose of the corporation. Humans do not always recognize their own stated purpose. Think about how great it would be if more people expressly knew what their stated purposes were. Imagine people operating their lives with a sense of purpose and an understanding of why they exist. It is frightening how much more mankind could accomplish if more people recognized the meaning of their existence. Victor Frankel analyzed "Man's Search for Meaning" but he probably never considered that corporations could serve as an example to men and women when it comes to assessing one's purpose or meaning. Corporations have it in writing. They do not have to search for meaning. Advantage, once again, corporations.

Do you see a pattern here? I am not saying that corporations are better than people. You should be able to come to that conclusion on your own. Can anyone understand why I have devoted so much more of my practice to representing businesses such as corporations rather than individuals? Because everything that a corporation stands for and everything a corporation is supposed to be is put in writing in the beginning, corporations are easier to deal with than individuals. You have a better idea of what you are getting into with a corporation as opposed to what is not exposed when you meet an individual for the first time.

Moreover, corporations need the intervention of others and a meeting and consultation in order to initiate changes. This opens the door for conflict amongst the people involved in the corporation if there is no agreement. However, the corporation is not a party to the conflict. The corporation will not fight to change or to not necessarily change. The corporation merely waits for the people who care about it to decide what changes to implement if any. When changes are made, they are reduced to writing so that the people dealing with the corporation from the outside can deal accordingly.

For example, let us imagine that a corporation's original articles provide that any leases or lease renewals must be ratified by the unanimous consent of the board of directors. That would mean that any landlord or potential landlord needs a copy of the unanimous consent executed by the board of directors in order to know that the corporation's lease is binding. But, if the articles are changed to reflect that only a majority of directors are required to ratify a lease renewal because there simply are too many directors, then all a landlord needs is a consent signed by the majority of directors. The landlord does not have to deal with every director. Once he or she knows that the majority of directors have approved a lease, he or she can assume that the lease will be binding upon the corporation despite the knowledge that one director was dead set against it.

As you think about it, the written books and records that constitute a corporation frame and define what the corporation is and how it will operate. The books and records are a contract amongst the people involved in the corporation as to what each party will do and what each party will get in exchange for what it does. The authority of the shareholders, directors and officers are established in writing. The written books and records provide focus and control. Anyone who acts outside of what the corporation's charter provides can be stopped. Anyone who is not on the same page as what the corporation is about cannot take the corporation in a direction contrary to what the written charter provides.

We mere humans would benefit from having such indispensable documentation to guide us in our lives. Another exercise to try would be to prepare for yourself a written charter and identify in writing all that you stand for and what you intend to do in order to achieve your stated purpose. Then, every time you face a conflict, refer to your charter. It would be difficult. It would require discipline. It might require creativity. But most importantly, it would require commitment.

Commitment is the toughest part of anything that must be done. If you can commit to your goals in writing however, think about how focused you could become. Face it, we all have made New Year's resolutions but can you remember the last one you made? Probably not. Did you keep the resolution? Probably not. Did you write it down and show it to others so that you could not renege? Definitely not. A written New Year's resolution shown to others would force you to have to at least think about keeping it. If you fail to keep it, someone will know. Because so few of us possess the discipline to police ourselves regarding our resolutions, it might benefit us to write them down, show them to others and be that much more motivated to follow through.

Because the charter of a business provides a written resolution as to what the business will stand for and what it hopes to achieve, you might reach the conclusion that businesses are better than people. If you do, you might be right. More importantly, if you realize the benefit of written commitments in the form of the books and records of a business, then you can appreciate a level of commitment that is significantly higher than what we mere humans might hold for ourselves. It is a level of commitment that entrepreneurs should try to adopt. The things we say we tend to forget, the things we write seldom let us fail to remember.

CHAPTER 22
I'm Vice President and General Manager.
But really, what's in a name?

Think about some of the titles we give to various people in business. For example, in the film industry, there is a title given to people who are "producers." The question to ask is what is a "producer?" In the film industry a "producer" is a person who takes a pile of money, a budget and an idea and employs people, equipment and technology to make a completed film that costs more than what was in the original pile of money.

Meanwhile, in the music industry, a producer is a person who blends a song, an artist, musical instruments, egos and technology to make a recording.

Meanwhile, in the real estate industry, a producer is a person capable of generating potential buyers for any particular property that is or could be for sale.

The point is that if a person in a particular industry has a title, you should find out what that title does and what it means. Find out who works under that title and who works with it. Then, once you assess what that title means and does, try to determine what character traits and attributes a person assuming that title needs. That way, you can make certain that you are employing the right person for the job.

Remember when we talked about banking in Chapter 11. Walk into any bank and you will meet a Vice President. They might be the Vice President of Financial Matters or Vice President of Transactions or simply Branch Vice President. Chances are that 95% of all people working for banks carry a title with the phrase "vice president" in it.

The truth is that titles are doled out in businesses with little or no regard for what they mean. My wife is a "Director" at a hospital but she is not on the board of directors for the hospital. I have a client who is an "operations supervisor" and all he does is load paper in a machine and press a button. My first job was working as a recreational baggage manager but the golfers just called me "caddy." The titles today are far removed from actually describing the job or function that the person performs. To that point, job titles today are really useless. It is as if you had a bag of labels and a bag of products. Now turn out the lights and put the labels on the products. You would have to get lucky to get the right labels on the right products. That is how titles are being thrown around in companies today. They are put on people by other people who are in the dark.

How did this happen? This happened because the assumption by the business community is that the buying public and employees are color blind to the distinctions signified by titles. We consumers, customers and employees do not think about the title. We just like the way it sounds. I had a problem with my phone bill so I called and reached an account manager who put me in touch with a department supervisor. When I asked the person what department he supervised I was put on hold and then, the phone went out. My service was restored two days later when I guess they figured that I had learned my lesson. "Don't pose questions to the phone company! You got it?"

The problem that this causes however is that we still ascribe some meaning to titles. We consumers, customers and employees make certain assumptions based on these meaningless titles. If someone is a supervisor, we assume that they have people who they supervise. If someone is a manager, we assume that they manage something. If someone is a "Department Head" then we assume that they are in charge of some department. The term Vice-President always sounds important. Being too loose with the titles we give to people causes people to make wrong assumptions about the titleholder. What's next? Calling the last place little league team "Vice-Champions" just because they finished the season?

The question you have to ask yourself in your business is what titles do you and your people have and do those titles adequately describe what you and your people do? I have an assistant in my office. She assists me. Some would say that she saves me. That is true most of the time but the term "assistant" most closely describes what she does as opposed to "savior." We could add the word "administrative" to her title because much of what she does is administrative. I have not deemed her vice-president of administrative affairs because that is too much title to fit on a business card and it implies that we have a president of administrative affairs.

The underlying reasons for doling out all these inaccurate titles are not all bad. They make people feel good. Some employers feel that giving someone a title is an inexpensive way of saying no to a raise or providing some level of appreciation for an employee. These might be good reasons. But the reasons do not necessarily justify the problems that they cause.

Perhaps the biggest problem caused by inaccurate titling of jobs is that it affects the thinking of people. The thought in a customer's mind as a result of talking to a vice-president is that they spent time with someone who has actual authority on behalf of the business to help the customer. I once called an 800 number to get help with some software I had installed and I talked to a "Customer Specialist." I kid you not. After about three minutes of describing my problem, the "Customer Specialist" advised that she could not help me. She expressed that she typically did not work with people like me on these problems. I bought the stupid software and I thought that made me a customer. I thought that a customer with a problem was the kind of people who "Customer Specialists" would talk to and attempt to help. Instead, she informed me that I would have to talk to someone in technical support because she was there to answer questions for people who had questions about the software and were thinking about buying it. I advised her that people who are thinking about buying her software are not customers until they buy the software like I did. I told her that her real title should be "Prospective Customer Specialist." She told me that she was not a "prospective" customer specialist because she already was a customer specialist. She felt that she was not a "prospect" for the position she already had. I told her that "Prospective" described the customer and not the specialist. While I spent the next ten minutes explaining my point and recognizing that she did not get it, I uninstalled the software and found my receipt. Back to the store it went.

What if a supplier takes an order from a vice-president for a great deal of products and then the supplier learns that the vice-president had no actual authority to place the order. Anyone would think that a vice-president had some authority. The supplier will not be happy to find that the person they were dealing with had no authority. Worse yet, the supplier might be gun shy to take any orders from the business ever again. Can you blame them?

So, being fast and loose with titles can be problematic. You need to avoid it no matter how good your intentions. More importantly, you need to recognize that titles communicate things about your business and your employees. As with everything else, you should strive to be accurate in your communicating.

CHAPTER 23
The Difference between "What are you Doing?"
And "What do you Do?"

Anyone who reads the questions can tell that there is a difference. "What are you doing?" implies that someone wants to know what actions or functions are you currently performing or what is your current position or title. "What do you do? Implies that someone wants to know what functions you perform and in some contexts, what is your title. Regrettably, as easy as it is to understand the difference between the two questions, many times in answering one someone actually answers the other.

Typically we hear the question. "What are you doing Scott?" Being a wise ass, I answer, "breathing." They seem confused at how simple I am. "No Scott, what we mean is what are you doing now?" Although my answer should be the same, I help them out by saying, "I'm the president of a corporation." Now here is where the problem lies. They did not ask me what job I hold. They asked me what I am doing. I should answer, "I am running a corporation." Then they will ask me the right question, "So you're the president?" And I answer "yup, sure am."

Other people ask "What do you do?" Again I answer that I breath. Then they ask, "for a living?" I answer, "yes, I breath for a living. I fear that if I stop breathing, I will no longer be living." I do not need a medical journal to confirm that I am correct about this.

I see the difference between the two questions as one of big picture versus details. The question "What are you doing?" should be answered in general terms. You should answer that by expressing what is your profession or what is your position. The gerund "doing" implies an act being done continually over some period of time. For that reason, your answer has to be general enough to encompass all the things you do in operating your business or in performing your job.

"What do you do?" is a more focused question. You can answer this by expressing what precise work you carry out. You might even describe what you do on a daily basis. You should think of this question as really being asked like this: "What specifically do you do?" In this context, your answer is tied to a more limited time frame of what your particular tasks are each day.

The reason the two questions are important is because you need to be able to know when to ask each question of yourself and you need to know how to answer each, In answering "What are you doing?" you should be able to express what is the more global reason for your work. For example, your answer might be, "I am a grain distributor." That answer lets you concentrate on what you ultimately do and hope to continue to do. If asked what you do, you answer, "I arrange for the resale and transport of grain products to major food suppliers throughout the Midwest." Then, by recognizing that you do this day in and day out and by accomplishing this you can say that you are a grain distributor. It is a forest and trees distinction. You need to see that what you are doing is part of the forest and what you do is part of the individual trees.

Once you comprehend the distinction, no matter how slight it is, you need to know when to ask yourself each question. Sometimes, answering one can help you accomplish the other. Sometimes you need to answer one in order to gain perspective about the other. If you say that you are an auto parts wholesaler then you have answered the question what are you doing. Recognizing that at the end of each day that is what you ultimately will be and that being that is your ultimate goal, your day is easier to manage. You simply do not need to do things that do not accomplish the more general description of what you are doing. So if you are an auto parts wholesaler, you do not actually service cars yourself. If asked to do that, you can look at what you do ultimately and say no. It is not what you do. In this way, your ultimate "big picture" description of what you do can keep you focused and can help you avoid the distraction of what you do on any particular day.

From this example, you might say, "but why not service a car if you are asked to do it? If you are capable of fixing a car, then why not perform that service?" The reason that you should not, even if it would be profitable, is that it causes you to lose direction. Everything you do in your day should be focused on furthering what you are ultimately doing. Do not dabble in things that are not part of what you are doing in the more global sense. Dabbling is nothing more than giving into distractions. Dabbling usually entails taking detours when you do not have to. Dabbling can be a waste of time.

Does this mean that you should never do something on the side? No, side jobs and things that you do outside of your routine are fine but do not let them take over unless you are willing to change the answer to the question "what are you doing?" If the side jobs offer more promise than what you are doing, then you might need to change your answer to what you are doing. If you enjoy those tasks more and you are prospering performing those tasks, then commit to them and change what you are doing. Change your forest to accommodate your new trees.

Otherwise, use your answer to what you are doing in order to give focus to what you do. From time to time stop and assess what you do during your day. If what you do helps you accomplish what you are ultimately doing then you are fine. If you do something that is not in line with what you are ultimately doing then you need to stop and refocus.

Delegating: The Right Person for the Right Job or, Having Doers help in what you are Doing.

The need to appreciate the distinction between what you are doing and what you do is not only important for yourself. It is important for your staff. Having people working for you who know what you are ultimately doing can keep them focused just as it keeps you focused. Once your personnel can share that focus, you can share the work load with them. Essentially, once your staff members can appreciate what your business is doing, then they can be told what things they need to do.

You should realize that until you can differentiate between what you are doing and what you do and potentially need to do to perform your function, you cannot learn to delegate authority to others and thereby let your business grow.

There is a big word for you: "delegate." Sounds like it is important, right? Do you know why? Probably because it is. Delegating is one of the most important functions and skills of an entrepreneur interested in growing the business beyond just his or herself. Notice I said it is a function and a skill. It is a function because it is a job, task or chore that needs to be done. It needs to be regarded as you would other necessary tasks and chores. It needs your commitment to assure its completion.

Delegation is also a skill. An entrepreneur who is accomplished at delegating can assess people's capabilities and can distribute tasks and assignments amongst people capable of carrying out those tasks and assignments. Most people respect the fact that this is not easy. Being able to recognize the capabilities of personnel is one thing but being able to delegate authority to the best person able to carry out an assignment is another. It requires that you be able to match people to assignments in order to maximize the likelihood of success of the assignment while also utilizing the individual to the best of his or her abilities.

Developing the skill takes experience and an investment of time and effort in learning about your personnel. It requires communication with your staff. It requires an ability on your part to read people. It requires an appreciation of what it takes to accomplish the tasks you are delegating. That is one of the reasons that the people who are best at delegating are usually the people who have worked in every phase of a business. Having done the tasks that one is delegating, they can appreciate what it takes to accomplish the task and they can choose the people to do the task based on the knowledge of what the task entails.

Delegation is a common function carried out in millions of small businesses everyday. An operator of a small business who can not handle everything that needs to be done by himself or herself must delegate to others. In delegating to others however, you should reinforce what the business is ultimately doing. You should make certain that the people you assign to carry out a task or job appreciate what you are ultimately doing.

For example, let us say that what you are doing is manufacturing radios and you assign a person to produce components to be installed in the radios. The person you delegated the job to manufactures the components and then calls a friend in the business who would like to buy all the components your company can make. The person you delegated the job to feels so proud for having sold all the components he made for the company. However, you wanted to have someone who knows not to sell the components he or she produces to someone else after they are completed. Selling the components is not what you company is doing. Producing the components is what the person you assigned that task is to do. Nothing more, nothing less. You might appreciate the ambition of the person for thinking about selling them but your company needs them. The employee did not realize what the company was doing. He did not seem to understand that the components he was producing were to be used for the company's final product. His desire to sell the components was not consistent with what the company is doing.

From this example, it seems that you need to make certain that the people to whom you delegate authority and tasks are on the same page in realizing what the company is ultimately doing. They need to know how what they do fits into what the company is ultimately doing. They need to know how their particular trees fit into your entire forest. And the only way that they can know is for you to know the difference between what you are doing and what you do.

CHAPTER 24
There are two things that happen that result in partnerships breaking up:
Success and Failure

Funny thing about partners, the good ones can survive mediocrity but the best ones learn to survive prosperity. It is a strange irony that when a business that involves more than one person, be it a partnership, or a corporation with only two or three stockholders or a small LLC, that these businesses break up when they achieve success. It seems that once things are going well and the business is doing well for its owners, the owners can no longer get along and it becomes necessary for them to go their separate ways and break up the profitable business. In some cases, that can be a good thing. The Beatles broke up when they were on top.

Now in all fairness, businesses that are struggling tend to break up as well. Usually, however, the fights are not as bad between the shareholders or partners because there is little or nothing in the pie pan to split up. It does not take a lot of emotion or thought to walk away from a failing business. Oftentimes people split with their partners from a failing in business with little or no animosity. For all but the few attorneys who like to bilk the split up, it is nice to see partners in a failing business acknowledge the failure and agree to walk away and maintain the friendship. As regrettable as it is that the business failed, I savor the occasions when in spite of the failure everyone agrees not to go to court to fight over the ashes. You would be surprised at how many failed business partnerships are unable to pay their attorneys.

For the other types of situation involving the break up in a failed business, there is animosity. Typically, businesses that split up because of success or failure have one thing in common. The break up over blame! The difference between the two comes down to who is to blame. In a failing business, the determination is that your partner screwed up and he or she is to blame for the business failing. So, rather than work harder, you decide that you want to unhitch your wagon from the donkey you thought was a work horse. In failing businesses, the person to blame is always the other guy.

Meanwhile, in the successful partnership, the person to blame is yourself.

> "I am the reason that the business is doing well. I am carrying my partners and I resent them for riding my coattails. They are profiting from my hard work and they are doing nothing to help me. As I think about it, I really do not need them. After all, look at all the success I am having in business with them as my anchor chains. I could prosper even more without them. That does it. I am going to break the partnership up. (Then, I hope that they say: Where is Scott's number?)."

In blaming yourself for the unbridled success of the business, you tend to forget that you could not have opened the business without the bank loan that was secured by your partner or without the cash that he or she brought in. You forget that your partner had the connections to bring in the major customer who accounts for half of the business. You forget to blame your partner for installing the computer software that he or she designed that resulted in an increase of sales and profitability. You are right to forget these things. You made the business all by yourself. It is now time to brush that pesky partner off of your coattails and leave them in your wake.

I love when these people come into the office to consult about winding up the company or partnership. They have an incredible way of explaining away all of the contributions of their partner. The way in which they delve deep into themselves to completely disregard what their partners have done is fascinating. By the time they get done, the only question I have to ask them is why did they ever hitch their wagon to such a useless slug in the first place. The answers are usually the same. "I felt sorry for the guy." And I think to myself, yup, when it all started there was this poor guy with a bundle of money just waiting to link up with the person sitting in my office. He had an idea for a business and he luckily met Mr. Wonder Partner who after using the money to make the business take off and probably even drawing a salary, now feels that he helped out the money

140

partner out of pity. And when I ask if the other partner will be expecting the return of their original cash investment in the partnership I get the same answer. "Why would they expect that? You see Scott, I am expecting that the current cash in the partnership will be divided at least 50/50. Maybe I should get more really. Do you understand what I'm saying?" And I am the nasty guy who drops the bomb on them. I have to tell them. "Well sure, I understand. But, here in reality, the party that made the original cash investment would probably expect to take the amount of the cash investment off the top before splitting what is left? In most cases, that is what courts refer to as 'fair."

The client then looks at me with a blank stare and some disappointment. "Why would my partner expect that? You see Scott, if that's how you're thinking, then maybe I should find another lawyer. The money was not what was important. It was me. It was all me. If you cannot understand that then maybe I should get another lawyer." And I respond, "I think you should. By the way, give my card to your partner because I would much prefer to represent him in this matter than you. Because at some point, in this real world of ours, your partner is going to get some, if not all, of his original investment back. You on the other hand, have no appreciation for your partner and you will have even less for me as your attorney who is telling you how things work in the world of business. I hope that this helps you. That will be $225.00!" And people wonder why lawyers are hated so much! Day in day out, it sucks to have to tell the truth to wide eyed optimists who think that their partners realize that they gave nothing but money to the partnership and only the contribution of their partner made the business profitable. The money they put up did nothing. Why those money partners are lucky that someone like Mr. Wonder Partner even took their money in the first place.

It is sad really when people cannot appreciate one another. It is even sadder when they cannot appreciate their lawyers in this lawyer's opinion. But apart from the appreciation issue, there is a real loss of reality by some people in these situations. Losing reality can be dangerous in the operation of a business. Entrepreneurs need real facts in order to make decisions. Distortions of those facts can lead to bad decisions. These bad decisions are not the result of faulty logic but are more often than not, the result of invalid assumptions.

Bad decision making, in this context, is especially apparent when there is bad delegation of assignments and projects at a business. When someone's ego gets way out in front of them and he or she begin to believe that they are more capable than they really are, that person risks undertaking something that they cannot do. If the person had realistically assessed what they were capable of doing in the first place, then the person may have decided to let another party perform the task.

Schultz & Smith was an up and coming print shop lead by its two principals. Smith was the printer technician and Schultz was the bookkeeper. Working in their respective capacities, they got along fabulously and the business did very well. On rare occasion they would have a small dispute but, for the most part, they had nothing major. After things started going very well, Schultz expressed that he needed to take some time off. Smith resented it at first but he agreed to let his partner take the time off. Schultz did have someone he trained to work the books in his stead. Smith resented this even more. After a short time, Smith became frustrated when the person filling in for Schultz limited Smith's ability to purchase certain materials. The person was doing nothing that Schultz had not done on many occasions. The person wanted to wait until there was enough cash available to get a discount for the supplies rather than pay the full price plus interest for the period that they needed credit.

The refusal to let Smith do something that Schultz would have also stopped him from doing did not sit well with Smith. So, feeling rather angry at the situation and feeling that he could handle things, Smith fired Schultz's substitute and Smith tried to juggle the books himself. Anyone with experience with these types of situations can take a sniff. Do you smell that? That is the smell of impending disaster.

Smith bought the supplies and overpaid. In handling the books, Smith fell behind in getting the invoices out. Soon the bill for the supplies came due and there was not enough money in the company account to pay. So credit was extended. Typically, in the past, on the rare occasions that this would have happened, Schultz would have given his own money to the company, interest free, in order to cover the short fall. Now the company would be paying for the supplies without the discount and paying interest on top of that. To add insult to injury, the supplier started spreading a rumor that the company was struggling because it usually paid on time within the discount period. Smith had cost the company money and had hurt its reputation in the industry all as a result of his own inability to recognize his lack of ability.

This scenario is typical. It is sad but it is also typical. Smith overestimated his own value to the company and his own ability and failed to appreciate the importance and complexity of what his partner did. Despite otherwise being successful, the company was hurt as a result. If you were to ask Smith though, he would insist that it was not his fault.

What can be done in these situations? Well in working with others in a business it is best to clearly delineate what each of the partners is doing. Identify what each of your roles will be and try, as best as possible, to keep to your area of responsibility. Focus on your part in the success of the company. Let your partner do what they do and try not to interfere. Also, make sure that they do not interfere with you. In this manner, you can easily determine where there are problems when things do not go smoothly. Blame will be attributed to the proper parties in these situations.

In addition, learn to appreciate your partners. To a greater or lesser extent, be grateful to them for putting up with you. One of the best ways to show gratitude is to put up with them during their troubled times. Build one another up from time to time.

Also, carry your weight. Show your partners that you are willing to push yourself to be successful in the business. Kick yourself in the ass from time to time. If you can push yourself then depending upon what you know about your partner, you can kick them in the ass as well. Root for them to be successful in what they do as you do your best in what you do.

Finally, commit not only to the business but to your partner as well. Never forget that each of you is trying to make a living and each of you wants the business to succeed. Do not compete with one another. Share in your mutual success and share blame for failures.

A great deal of this probably sounds elementary or even banal to some of you. If it is then so be it. For those of you who are not too egotistical, however, it probably sounds like common sense.

PART IV Getting Over _____

CHAPTER 25
Getting over Losing a Customer

So you lost a customer. Your response to this proposition says a lot about you. If your answers is, "so" then the customer probably did not mean a whole lot to you. If your answer is. "oh my God, what am I going to do, this is the end of the business . . " then this customer meant too much to you. Any good customer deserves some element of concern on your part and therefore the first answer is not indicative of a proper attitude. Nevertheless, the latter answer is indicative of a relationship that has gotten out of control. In that response you have shown that your business was revolving around only that customer. You hitched your wagon to one horse and now that horse is gone.

Chances are, if you are bothering to read this chapter, then your answer was not: "so?" You probably care about your customers and losing any one of them is a concern. That is a sign of a healthy business attitude. You should be concerned about your customers. If you lose one, you should care. You need to keep the loss in perspective however. The loss needs to be analyzed and not obsessed over. Your focus should be on why did you lose the customer and not what will it do to the business.

In assessing why you lost the customer, you need to do some market research. Marketing is not only about finding new customers it is about assessing the needs of all customers even the ones you lose. Moreover, it is about finding out about why you might be losing them. Good marketers use information about customers in an industry to tailor an individual business to the needs and wants of the customers. If a customer is leaving you, then you need to ask why. Some customers might not tell you. Do not read anything into why they did not tell you. Try to figure out what happened but do not base any decisions you make on suppositions or assumptions. Your assessment should only be based on facts. If you cannot find any facts, then your assessment stops. You do not have to think about why you lost that customer if you cannot find any facts supporting their decision not to continue doing business with you.

Most customers that leave you will tell you why. Some might have a laundry list of complaints about you. If they do, then listen. Consider each complaint. Assess what complaints are based on facts and which ones might merely reflect personal feelings. Then distinguish which ones you can do anything about from those that you cannot do anything about. For example, the customer might have the following complaint: "your company does not do internet invoicing and we want to do all of our business over the internet." If none of the rest of your customers require internet invoicing, and the cost of learning anew system would be cost prohibitive to accommodate only this one customer, then you cannot do anything about this complaint or about losing that customer. If you are a pizza place and the customer moves out of your delivery area, you cannot do anything about that. Some customers you just lose.

In these cases, you need to look at the customer as an individual. Consider why the customer is no longer doing business with you. Is the customer going out of business? If so, is it your fault? Is the customer relocating? Is that your fault? Has the customer's business changed and now they no longer need your services or products? If so, is that your fault?

After considering the customer's individual circumstances you always have to ask if your at fault for losing the customer. You need to look at yourself. Introspection is the best way to analyze why relationships do not last. Did you do all that you could for the customer? Is the customer leaving because of something you did or did not do? Has your company's or your attitude changed in some way? Has your company's personnel changed and is that affecting the relationship? Is there anything you can do to try to get the customer to return?

In too many cases, some entrepreneurs are never willing to blame themselves. No one ever wants to blame themselves. But, in business, you have to accept that you are not perfect. If you can accept your ability to be less than perfect then you can acknowledge failure. If you can recognize that with some customers you can fail then you can perform an honest assessment as to why you lost a customer. If you cannot be honest about the assessment then it is not worth doing.

Honesty is said to be the best policy. In fact, honesty should not be a policy at all. It is instead a perspective. You need to look at things honestly without concern for your personal feelings, attitudes or sensitivities. If you are at fault for something, you need to have an honest perspective about it and you need to blame yourself. Perhaps you did do something to lose the customer's business. Maybe it was your fault or maybe it was not. The point is that one of the only benefits you can gain from losing a customer is performing an honest assessment as to why and, if you are at fault, then trying to fix it for that customer or for your other customers.

As preached throughout this book, do not go overboard. Do not go to the extreme. Blaming yourself does not mean beating yourself up. Blaming yourself only means holding yourself accountable and not completely undermining your confidence or thinking badly of yourself. Once again, put things into perspective. If you failed, acknowledge the failure, assess why it happened and try to avoid the things that lead to the failure in the first place.

In assessing why you might have lost a customer you also need to realize that your business and the customer shared a relationship. Relationships need to be studied. The essential ingredient to any relationship is that it involves more than one party. Being honest with yourself can help you to assess your part in any relationship with a customer. But, in studying the relationship, you also need to study the customer as the other party to the relationship and. more importantly, what the customer gains from the relationship. Then you need to look at what you gain from the relationship. What is the mutuality that the relationship is based upon? What does your business do for the customer and what does the customer mean to you? This type of analysis is called "taking stock in your customers."

Taking Stock in Your Customers

Think of your customers as stocks. The time and effort you put into serving them is your investment. Once you analogize your thinking of customers in this way then all the standard investment strategies apply. In managing your portfolio of customers or clients, you should consider what your long terms and short terms goals are. Are you willing to take greater risks in order to possibly attain greater gains or are you more conservative?

Are you willing to work for customers who can do a great deal of very profitable business with you but, it might not last or they might not be able to pay you or are you more focused on customers who only have the highest credit rating but only can send you a limited amount of business that has a small profit margin?

In determining investment strategy, perhaps the most important question to ask is, "is my portfolio diversified?" Diversification of your portfolio is one of the most important investment strategies. Have you applied it to your business? In your portfolio does any one stock or fund account for almost all of your investments? In your business, does any single customer account for almost all of your receivables?

The more diversified your customer base, the more you will feel that you are in business for yourself. The less diversified, or in essence, the fewer the number of customers you have, the less you will feel that you are in business for yourself. Face it, if you have only one big customer and you are not interested in expanding your customer base, then you are really just working for someone. The only difference between your business having one big customer and you being employed is that you are paying for your own benefits. You are completely dependent on that customer. Your business is sensitive to any whim of that customer. If they need something in the middle of the night, you have to perform. If they want to discuss your prices, you have to listen.

Meanwhile, if you have hundreds of customers and any one says that they want you to reduce your prices, you really do not have to listen. If that customer accounts for such a small percentage of your total revenue, then you really do not have to be sensitive to that customer's unwillingness to pay. You have sufficient demand at the prices you set to not have to worry about that customer. If a customer is complaining about prices, you should note it for future reference either about the customer or to see if it is just the first in a long line of complaints. Then, until you have more complaints or until that customer can bring you so much business as to warrant listening, you can tune it out.

In summary, losing any customer should be a troubling event but it should not be traumatic. If it is a customer that accounts for too significant a total of your entire revenue, then it will be traumatic. In those cases, you need to consider diversifying. You need to commit to establishing a customer bases that is spread out enough so as to not "bet the business" on just the one customer. The problem with being too dependent upon just one customer is that in doing so, you link your business' fate to that customer. You also become nothing more than an employee with that customer as your only boss.

Another investment strategy is based on confidence analysis. Can you purchase a stock with some element of confidence in its eventual profitability or will you have to constantly monitor it and commit time and effort to endlessly researching it. Some customers are like that. Can you simply do business with them and reasonably expect them to be satisfied and, more importantly, pay? Or do you need to endlessly spend time and effort assuring that the customer is satisfied and endlessly calling the customer for money? Customers like this, much like stocks that you cannot be confident about, can cause you unnecessary stress and can tap your energy. The amount of time that you spend monitoring a customer and calling to get paid digs into the profit margin you make on that customer. If you cannot trust that a customer you have worked for will be satisfied or will pay, then you need to evaluate the real value of that customer. As with stocks that do not inspire confidence, you might need to divest.

Another investment strategy is market and trend analysis. You not only need to watch your particular stock but you have to keep an eye on the industry in which the stock is competing. In the same way, you need to have a feel for what is going on with your customers. Is your customer doing okay? Are they profitable? If they are not making money, you need to assess their ability to pay you. If they cannot pay you then do you mind losing them as a customer? What if they are in a short term cash crunch because they are developing a new product that will be revolutionary and extremely profitable? Only by looking at the trends and the market where the customer is competing can you evaluate whether or not you want to keep the customer.

Once you have applied investment strategies to your evaluation of your customers you can gain a better perspective when you lose one. In assessing each customer like they are an investment you can determine which ones are worthy of your investment and which might not be so bad to lose. The point is to not obsess over losing anyone customer. If the customer was profitable to you then the loss hurts more. But, if the customer was not easily satisfied and did not pay you too well and was always trying to take advantage and needed an extraordinary amount of your time, then losing that customer should be a blessing. All you need to feel bad about is what that customer is going to do to your competitor who goes after it. And that does not feel so bad.

Conveying Your Message so as not to Lose Customers

Still you remain determined not to lose any customers. Well if after doing your investment analysis you still find that you want certain customers then the burden falls on you to take steps to try to keep your customers. Getting over losing a customer can best be accomplished by reestablishing a bond with your remaining customers so as not to let the loss become pandemic. You need to determine what you convey to your customers about your business. What is the message you are sending to your customers about how important they are to you.

The real trick is trying to make each of your customers feel as important as if they were your only customer. You might not want to let them think, however, that they are your only customer because that might cause them to feel that they have the advantage in dealing with you. They might take you for granted. Let them think that you are busy with a great many customers. If they are savvy business people, they should respect that. It should give them some perspective in dealing with you. But, try to balance that against making sure that they never feel that you are too busy for them. When doing something for them, make them feel as if they are the most important customer for your business at that particular moment. They will not be thinking about you 24/7. They will think about you when they need you so when they need you show them that you are thinking about them. They should not expect that you think about them 24/7 but they should expect you to give them undivided attention for the times when they are your paying customer.

If you have honestly done everything that you can to convey to your customers that they are important to you and that you are committed to their satisfaction, then losing one should not be a problem. Either they will not leave you or if they do, it probably will not be your fault. And if it is not your fault anyway, get over it.

CHAPTER 26
Getting over Losing a Valued Employee

Losing a valued employee can be devastating. It should not be however. It should not be devastating from an emotional standpoint and it should not be devastating economically. It can be sad. It might be inopportune. It could be regrettable and unfortunate. But, you should not let it be devastating. If it is devastating, then you are doing something wrong. You are developing the wrong type of relationship with your employees. You might also be developing too great a dependence on your employees.

No one ever wants to lose an employee who they have trained and who they like. That is an unfortunate event. But, to the extent that it becomes devastating, you may have failed the business in some way by not establishing the proper relationship with the employee.

We talked before in Chapter 8 about how employees are different from you. We talked about how you have to be productive and that you have to endure the constant stress of having to perform and make money. We talked about how employees really only need to do the minimum necessary to keep their job. They have to do nothing more, nothing less. You need to recognize that an employee's goal should be maintaining their job enough so as to obtain his or her paycheck. Your goal is to maintain the business in order to make enough money to cover payroll. What makes you different is that you have to always be committed to do everything you can to make as much money as possible.

In order to make as much money as possible, you need to make your employees as productive as you possibly can while paying them the minimum that they are willing to accept to be that productive. This sounds cold but it is an essential economic principle. Your ability to manage people is only as good as your ability to utilize their efforts on behalf of your business so as to maximize your profits.

But what about those rare employees who you genuinely like to work with and who work hard for your business? What about the ones who are dedicated and loyal? The best thing you can do for them is show your appreciation. Cherish them and tell them that you do. If they do well for the company, then recognize their value to you and give them bonuses and raises to entice them to stay. Do what you can to reciprocate in your business relationship. Moreover, if they are truly dedicated, then put them in a profit sharing program. Offer to sell stock in the business to them if they appear to be the type of person you want as a fellow shareholder. If you have an employee who displays an extraordinary commitment then you should consider doing something to show them your commitment to them.

The important thing to do, however, is to evaluate why the employee is valuable to you. If they are more productive than you could have hoped when you hired them and you do not want to lose them, then have the business do things for them in order to prevent, to the extent possible, losing them. If you merely like having them around but they are not as productive as you would want, then you have a problem. Now you have a balancing act problem. Liking having a particular employee around without assessing the employee's productivity is indicative of a personal relationship. The business can have only one type of relationship with the employee. To the business, the employee is no different from any piece of capital such as a copy machine or packaging machine. To the business, the employee has to be productive. That defines the relationship. You cannot let your personal relationships with the employees interfere with the business's relationship with the employees.

Why the distinction between your personal relationship with the employees and the business's relationship with the employees? There is a one word answer. Money. You hired the person to help the business make money not to be your personal friend. If you are hiring people to be your friends, you have got some serious problems.

Think about it this way. Your employee is coming to work and expecting to get paid. They will not seem friendly if at the end of the work week instead of giving them a paycheck you tell them, "hey, I really appreciate you being a friend and helping me out this week. I don't have a check for you but, if there is anything you need from me someday, I will return the favor buddy." You have enough brains not to say this because you know that they worked for their paycheck. It is their expectation and you should satisfy that expectation. Do not ever forget that in having an expectation of receiving a paycheck, an employee is treating your relationship as a business. It is an economic relationship. They might feel it is a friendship but there is a distinction that you should understand that makes the relationship with employees very different from friendships.

Friendship is based on mutuality of concern for one another. There are no laws on the books to govern friendships. If I help a friend move into his new condo and spend a whole weekend doing it, I cannot sue him for the cost of my time. I did it to be a friend. I cannot even sue him if I ask him to help me move a year later and he refuses. I cannot sue for my right as a friend because such rights are not recognized under the law. You do things for your friends at your own peril. If they do not reciprocate than you should get better at picking your friend.

Employees, on the other hand, have rights that are enforced by specific agency in every state of the union as well as in the courts. If an employee works for you and you do not pay them, they can report you to the state's labor agency or department of employment to get paid as is their right to do. If they fall down and break their leg at work, they will file a worker's compensation claim as is their right to do as an employee. If you comment about how that blouse really accentuates their bosom, you can expect them to file a sexual harassment case against you as is their right to do. If you fire them, they will apply for unemployment benefits as is their right to do under the law. If you request that they work more than forty hours, they can decline as is their right to do under the law. A friend who is not your employee cannot sue you for not paying them or sexually harassing them or for worker's compensation. A friend cannot collect "unfriendship" benefits after you have ended your friendship. A friend has to merely chalk it up to the cost of being your friend.

There are other differences to the relationship your have with employees as opposed to relationships you have with friends outside of the differences in terms of legal rights. If you do not pay employees what they feel they are worth, they will take a job elsewhere. You cannot blame them. It would be an economic decision on their part. Maybe, they are pursuing a business opportunity that you cannot give them. Should they stay with you out of friendship? They might but they should not and you should not encourage them to. If you do, then you open yourself and the business up to being resented when they do not later fulfill their dreams.

The harsh reality is that the relationship you have with an employee, no matter how valuable, is not the same as the relationship you have with a friend. If you lose a friend, that can be emotionally devastating for you. But if your business loses an employee, you cannot let it be devastating. The business cannot afford to be that dependent upon any single employee. The business has a relationship with the employee that is more important than any personal feelings you might have for the employee.

Once again, this is a rather cold way of thinking about your employees. But, in learning to get over losing an employee, even a valued employee, this is the most effective way for you as an entrepreneur to get over it. You will suffer economic consequences as a result of losing highly productive employees but for the most part, you will figure out a way to get the work done. But if you are suffering some emotional damage as a result of losing a valued employee then you have blurred the line between employee and friend. Recognizing the difference between friends and employees in terms of legal and economic realities will help you to have the right perspective when, God forbid, you lose that valued employee. When you possess the right perspective, it will not be devastating and you will get over it.

CHAPTER 27
Getting over Losing Your Mind

Do not ask me why you opened your own business. I did not tell you to do it. Do not blame me if you read "Who Wants to be a Businessaire?" and thought that it might be fun to start your own business. If you read that book and still decided to open your own business, then you are pretty dense. That book was not about pushing you to open your own business. That book was about developing the "feel" of being in business for yourself.

This book is no different. It too is all about "feel." Now that you are already in business, this book is relating all sorts of concepts and experiences that you might be encountering. This book is about developing the "feel" for approaching the issues you will face or already are facing as you have no choice but to continue in business.

So again, do not ask me why you opened your own business. As I said, I did not tell you to do it. Chances are, no one told you to do it. You are the type of self motivated individual who moves forward with such things without really taking orders or advice from others. If people who opened their own businesses were the type of people who took advice, this would be a very different book. But because they are not docile or smart enough to listen to advice, I wrote a book that is not so much a "how to" as it is a "why are you?" This book is nothing more than my observations and condescending commentary about why small business people do the crazy things that they do.

So all of this being said, how do you get over losing your mind in business is not the question that should preoccupy you. You are in business already and that alone demonstrates that you have adequately lost your mind. You have not really listened to anybody to this point. You have been single minded and now you have lost that single mind. Too bad minds are not like kidneys or liver or some other organs. If your mind were like a kidney, you would have two and you could get a transplant if both were lost. If your mind were like a liver, you could get a small piece of someone else's and you could survive. Unfortunately, no one can give you a piece of their mind literally, Figuratively speaking notwithstanding, we only have one mind and you, the small business owner, lost yours.

So what are we really talking about here? Well we are talking about what happens when owning your own business becomes overwhelming. What happens on those days that you are convinced that you are losing your mind?

This chapter is not going to be a pep talk about how you can make it and about how I believe in you. You do not have time for that BS and I do not particularly care to blow sunshine up your skirt. More importantly, business people do not need some feel good therapy to get through those really bad days. If anything, that type of thing becomes counterproductive. A good dose of discipline is more likely to get you through those days. You need to be your own drill sergeant.

As your own drill sergeant, you may come to understand that you can deal with those days by recognizing that overcoming them is as much about attitude as it is about anything else. Those days make most of us adopt a crappy attitude. Sometimes, enough of those days in a row or in a short period of time make us feel like saying, "I don't care anymore!"

Unfortunately, when you are in business for yourself, you have to care. You could probably stop caring for a small while like ten seconds or so. Maybe you could stop caring during your lunch break. But, not caring is not a good long term strategy in your own business. That type of attitude seems to shine through everything. It obliterates past accomplishments in the eyes of your customers. After trying to get a customer back after mistreating them, you cannot rely on telling them that you did care about them before yesterday. The truth is, they are not going to understand. They want you to care about them every day.

So although those days usually make you adopt a bad attitude it is important that you not let that happen. You need to be disciplined enough to develop a good and healthy attitude. I am serious. I joke a great deal but about that, I am not kidding. Bad attitudes bleed through your clothes for everyone to see. You cannot hide them. This is why they become particularly dangerous to small businesses and the people who run them.

Let us look at a typical day and your typical attitude. If you are overwhelmed and all you do is say "too bad for those who I could not help but I am just too busy" well then you probably feel bad. As much as you try not to feel that way, you do feel some guilt over not being able to be perfect for everyone. Face it you little over achiever, you always strive to be perfect. When you cannot be perfect and always do the best for every customer or client, you feel bad. You might cover up your feelings about it but still you feel bad.

Would you like to feel better? If your attitude can be summed up by saying "too bad for those who I could not help but I am just too busy" then try a different statement. Try, "I regret that I cannot be perfect for everyone but I have really tried to help everyone I could." You are still not perfect but at least with this attitude, you can feel better. Do you want to better still? Try this, "I tried hard and helped everyone I was able to help today." And add to that, "I did not fail to help anyone who was not counting on me and was not worthy of my help." The last one shows a real "can do" spirit.

The important thing here is that despite feeling like you are losing your mind, you are focusing on the needs of your customers and of your business. Less thinking about yourself in these situations benefits everyone. When you face those days where you are losing your mind, thinking about yourself only leads to self pity anyway. There is little or no value in a self-pitying attitude so let it go. Think about how much you want to help, serve and sell to others. That is the reason why you are in business.

Perhaps the most important reason why you have to build and maintain a good attitude towards those really bad days is so that others will respect your leadership. Face it, it takes nothing to lead a company on a good day. Without the type of adversity that causes you to lose your mind, it is pretty easy to run your small business. While things are going well, you have little need for intense decision making and handling stress. It is easy to maintain your perspective in the more prosperous times. The problem is that prosperity is never a constant. You might have long periods of prosperity and good times, and you should relish them, but prosperity has a short shelf life for most small businesses.

This leads to the point that should be well understood by anyone who has run a small business for any significant length of time. The time to do something about the days that cause you to lose your mind is when things are going well. During the less stressful and potentially less hectic times that you will enjoy in your business from time to time, plan for those bad days. Use the more prosperous times to develop systems for when things go wrong. When money is coming in, set up a savings plan. When you have good people on staff, give them contracts, bonuses and/or raises. When a supply chain is working well, take advantage and stock up even more than usual. This may seem like rainy day planning because it is.

Now you are saying. "okay hotshot writer, what do I do on those days when I am losing my mind and all the planning in the world could not have prepared me for what I am encountering now!" You probably already know the answer but, in order to be fair to everybody, I will make it a little easier. Let us try a multiple choice test. Ready? Begin.

1. When things get tough, the tough get:
   a. Laid
   b. Drunk
   c. Welfare
   d. Some of the above
   e. Angry

2. What does it take to not lose your mind in your small business:
   a. Money
   b. More money
   c. Investors with money
   d. A firm understanding of the principles in this book
   e. Did we say money?

3. Things you should do as soon as you realize that you are losing your mind:
   a. Panic, vomit and defecate
   b. Answer a. is gross
   c. Read a good book such as "Who Wants to be a Businessaire?"
   d. Get your hair done before you pull it out
   e. Get laid, get drunk, apply for welfare and get angry

(The Answer Key: 1. f, 2. f., 3. f)

So how did you score? What does this demonstrate? It is intended to make all but the most serious of you laugh. The too serious are angrily trying to figure out why they did not get any right. Hey, Poindexter, or Poindextra if you are a female, get over it. It was a joke. You probably

157

have already lost your mind.

Laugh. It is important to do. Personally, I have always thought that we have a genuine biological need to laugh. I will wait for a study. The truth is that we need to laugh through some things and, in experiences that cause us to lose our minds, we need to laugh at the ridiculous lead character in our lives: ourselves.

So there you are. You are losing your mind. You are screaming, yelling crying and making a complete ass of yourself. You swear that you are losing your mind. This is the best time to laugh about it. Laugh at how ridiculous it is that you are screaming, yelling etc. What is so funny? It is both funny and ironic that for all the yelling, screaming and crying you are doing, each one of those actions is counterproductive to getting your mind back. I find it funny and ironic.

I never knew how ridiculous I was in running my practice on those really bad days until I considered videotaping myself. There I was on tape screaming, yelling throwing stuff, losing stuff as a result, breaking furniture and making everyone around me uncomfortable. My God I was being a jerk. I never realized how funny it was though until I watched myself. When I did that, I could not help but laugh. The idiot on that tape looked like he was three years old having a temper tantrum.

Now if you do not have a video camera, you can still watch yourself. Use a mirror or simply step out of yourself for a minute. Watch yourself crying uncontrollably as you realize that you cannot get something accomplished on time. Then, laugh about the fact that wasting time crying about it does nothing but make the goal that much more unattainable.

Since watching myself and how ridiculous I looked, I have implemented some changes. I have taken a step back and realized that those days that cause some people to lose their minds can happen and cannot always be avoided. I realized that I do not want to lose my mind however. If anything, I want to be the type of person who seems pretty cool under pressure. I do not want to watch myself being a jerk anymore. I want to be calm in the wake of crisis like a great leader should be.

This somewhat brings me back to my point from before. If I watched my video tape of me on a good day it would not be funny or even interesting. As I say, it takes nothing to run the business on the easy days. But, when I think about standing outside of myself and watching how I handle one those crisis laden days, I want to watch someone who is in control. I want to watch someone who I respect. I want to watch someone creatively attack the problems he is facing. I want to watch someone who is up to the challenges.

All of this made me realize one simple truth: Great leaders are not molded on good days, great leaders are forged on bad ones.

Think about it. If you opted to open and run a business you probably did so because you idolize great leaders. If you did not, then you would have been happy to continue as an employee. But if you chose to lead, even your own business, then you must have been inspired by someone who led in the past. And if you were inspired by that person then you can no doubt recall how well they did things in that leadership role.

As you think about how you have been inspired, think about being a great leader yourself. Great leaders do not ever look like they are losing their minds. Great leaders can handle adversity without crying on those really bad days. Great leaders approach adversity without losing their cool or losing control. They do not relent in the face of overwhelming odds. Sometimes they get mad and that gives them the spark to fight back. Great leaders do not fall into a rut with a bad attitude. Great leaders do not sit and feel sorry for themselves but instead, they put others' needs before their own. Great leaders can laugh at themselves because they do not lose perspective.

So now when you face one of those days when you fear that you are losing your mind, you can handle it. You can tell yourself that you cannot lose your mind because you are a great leader. You realize that you need to keep calm, put others first, keep a good attitude, laugh at yourself and maintain your perspective and do things the way that great leaders do them. Soon you will realize that the more days you have like that, the more you will have an opportunity to develop and be the great leader that you have idolized.

CHAPTER 28
Getting over Losing

The old adage "sometime you win sometimes you lose" certainly applies to owning and operating your own business. The other adage that is similar is " you win a few, you lose a few." That is true in small business. You probably do not always win and you do not have to always lose. Sometimes, even in your own small business you can enjoy a mixture of success and failure. The problem is that oftentimes losing is a prelude to more losing. You get into a funk of some sort whereby you cannot escape failure.

How does this "loser feeling" start? Over time you may start to feel that you lose more than you win. Perhaps you will begin to feel that you always lose. That is a possibility. You might in fact lose all the time. However, if you are open to the possibility of winning at least some of the time, then you can win a few. But, before we get to that, let us discuss the possibility of just pure losing and how that feels.

It seems ironic that in the business context the most problematic consequence faced by people who constantly lose is also the greatest threat to those who constantly win. That threat and consequence is: complacency. In a later chapter we will talk about the threat complacency poses to winners. But, for now, we are focusing on how complacency affects losers. In the opinion I have formed from numerous observations of people for many years, I have learned that business owners who manage their complacency and then overcome it, learn how to win consistently. Notice I said consistently and not always. Luck still plays a factor as does the amount of risk that any individual may take. But, if you remove complacency from the equation, you are likely to add more wins to your endeavors in business.

So how do people become complacent losers in business? My analysis, as always, is not psychological. My analysis is from anecdotal and historical evidence. One of the best anecdotes I can recall is the story of Colleen. She opened a business that seemed destined to succeed and became absolutely beset with failure. She became complacent and almost resolved to being a failure. Her story is not so unique.

Colleen opened a coffee shop on a reasonably busy corner in the suburbs. She did her homework and found a place near public transportation. She found a location that was visible but had low rent. She worked with suppliers who had reasonable prices and quality products. She hired very conscientious help usually consisting of working moms and college students who were available to work mornings but needed afternoons free. Overall, given that it was a nice cash business, she had put together a pretty nice set up. She had put together the ingredients for success.

At first, she enjoyed success. She developed a healthy business of regulars with occasional newcomers who would buy a cup of coffee to go on the way to the nearby public transportation. She maintained a pretty regular staff that appreciated the arrangements because the shop was not opened in the afternoons. Business was not exactly booming but she was making a profit.

After six months, however, a major coffee shop chain opened a space across the street. Being a major franchise, the competitor shop had a great many advantages. Its management and staff had been professionally and specifically trained to obtain maximum market share. It offered a competitive priced product that was of equal quality to that offered by Colleen. It had a much greater advertising budget. Its grand opening specials alone had undercut Colleen's prices below her costs.

After the new business opened, everything that Colleen tried to do failed. She tried specials that did not attract new customers and hardly kept the few remaining customers she had. She spent money on newspaper ads and coupons that proved a waste of money. She lowered prices and still nothing gave her a competitive edge.

As time went on, her competitor started to pouch Colleen's employees. She could not offer the same comprehensive benefits as the major franchise could so she lost them too. As a result of her three year lease, she could not close the business. Soon she was running the shop more or less by herself. She had such a small amount of business, running it herself was hardly a problem.

At first when things began going badly, she was depressed. She was down right despondent as she tried to think of ways to get back on top. She thought and thought and thought and still she could not come up with a solution. Then, over a short while, she was no longer depressed. She seemed to accept the fact that her business was failing. She put almost no effort into changing it. She felt that she could not win and she became complacent that she would have to keep open long enough to finish out her lease and then she would close. She would accept her losses and that would be that.

I stopped in to see her after the depression had ended and when she seemed resigned to her failure. She was hardly the same person who I had remembered opening the business. Awash in her failure and complacent that she could do nothing about it, she charged me $5.50 for a cup of coffee. Feeling sorry for her and having six dollars on me, I gave her all of it. I sat down and talked about how things were when she first opened. I talked about her dreams and how she executed her original plans so well. I told her that it was a bad break that her competitor had opened across the street.

She told me to stop trying to cheer her up. She expressed that I was pathetic at it. She told me to stop patronizing her and to stop being a patron of her shop if all I could do was feel sorry for her. She yelled at me in ways that would make my wife jealous. As she let me have it, it seemed as though she was slowly starting to feel more animated. She was becoming angry with me to the point that she told me to get the hell out of her shop. She had achieved some purpose in telling me off. It was as if telling me off recharged her batteries. It seemed that having me, whom she though of as pathetic, feeling sorry for her made her ashamed of feeling sorry for herself. She felt that if I had felt sorry for her, then she really did hit rock bottom.

Her attitude changed immediately. It was a profound moment for her. She was inspired. She immediately came to grips with her situation. She developed a plan. First, to replace her lost employees, she called her mother who had retired after many years of working part time in a restaurant. Colleen told her that it would be wise for her to keep the person destined to select her nursing home happy. That happiness would come from helping out her daughter at a crucial period. Her mother felt compelled to help her.

Then, Colleen started one of the most unique marketing campaigns I had ever seen up to that time. On a quiet morning when there were many customers in her competitor's store, she took a sling and propelled a cup of coffee at the front door of the competitor breaking the awning. She got arrested and the story made the newspapers and a local news broadcast. When asked why, she expressed that her actions were symbolic of David and Goliath. Her silly stunt was intended to show her competitor that she was willing to compete. She let customers know that she was the little guy. She positioned herself as the ultimate underdog. Then she changed her company motto and put it on her sign and business card. "Standing eye to eye with giants." When the competitor expressed that it would press charges, her statement was indeed made. As the story gained momentum, the competitor eventually decided not to press charges as it was only working against them and helping her.

Only in a world and time as perverse as ours could such a stunt work. So of course, it did. Patrons revisited her shop. New people came by who had heard about the story. Other similarly situated business owners came by to buy a cup of coffee and show some solidarity. People pull for an underdog and Colleen counted on that.

She enjoyed moderate success for a while after that. Soon, however, the public's memory of her stunt faded and the business began to slip again. By that time, however, she did not care. She met a wealthy customer and she married him. She moved into his big house and she whittled away her days spending the fortune he had inherited. In recognition of her mother's help, she let her move in (my suggestion) with them. Recognizing that it was my patronizing and condescension that inspired her to quit being a complacent loser and to fight her competitor and bring her shop back from the dead, Colleen continues to send me a Christmas card with the exact same sentiment expressed year after year: "Merry Christmas JERK!!!!" I assume that she means it affectionately. Her mother also sends me a card that says "Thanks." I like her mom. Colleen? Not so much.

The point to this story is that Colleen found a reason to overcome the complacency she felt in losing. She got mad. She set her mind to getting out of her rut. She took a risk. She did get arrested for it and she made that work for her. She went out and banked on sympathy. She turned sympathy into cash. Most importantly, she quit feeling sorry for herself. She found a creative way to succeed.

For business owners who find themselves becoming complacent with losing, you have the same chance as Colleen. Some of you might face monumental odds of eventually succeeding but you can at least overcome the complacency. There is value in telling yourself that you can try to fix things and that even if you lose time and time again, you can try to win. A guy might be a terrible golfer but if you put a blind fold on him and let him take 100 shots at a five foot putt, chances are, he will make a few. Think of it this way, odds are, he will make a few. Luck might have something to do with it but the mere act of trying at least allows for a chance at success.

Remember, when we say "trying" we mean legitimately trying. Going through the motions is not trying. Frankly, going through the motions on anything is more or less just a waste of time. There is a problem when the complacency you feel about losing creeps into your attitude about trying. It undermines the effort you actually put into trying. At that point, you are not really trying your hardest. You are merely going through the motions.

The other point about escaping the complacency of losing is to find inspiration. The complacency becomes compounded when you feel that anything you could eventually win is not all that important to you. You start to feel that why try to win anything because there is nothing worth winning. Eventually, you tell yourself, there is no point in putting in the effort to try to win.

When that happens, the prize for winning needs to be redefined. The prize needs to inspire your best efforts. In Colleen's case, she was taking satisfaction in succeeding in the face of my patronizing. That inspired her. In any other business person's case, the inspiration may come from any one of a number of sources. Perhaps you need to succeed to pay your bills. Maybe you need to win one particular customer over to open the door to many more. Maybe you need to succeed to compete with a spouse, a sibling, a friend or some other person. Maybe you just need it for yourself to show you that you can do it. The important thing is to enhance the value of the prize in your mind and then trying to win will result in you putting out your best efforts.

Lastly, do not look at losing as a pattern. This means you Cubs' fans. Losing happens. Sometimes it happens a lot. Sometimes there is no explaining it. But, in some cases, if it happens over a longer period of time, some people think that there must be a pattern. They begin to think that they are destined to lose. The problem for them is that over time, unconsciously, they make the pattern happen. On occasions when they can overcome their losing ways and finally have a chance to win, they undermine themselves. The reason is simple. After they have committed to the idea that they have developed this pattern of losing they begin to put too much pressure on winning. Trying to win anything results in a certain amount of pressure. Trying to win when you consider yourself a loser who ultimately "must" win in any given situation is overwhelming. It puts your competitor (like say the 2003 Florida Marlins) at an advantage because your competitor is facing the regular pressure of trying to win. You, on the other hand, are trying to overcome a self imposed pattern of losing by trying to win this particular game.

How do you overcome a losing streak? It really is simple. You need to consider some statistical analysis in order to put it into perspective. You need to recognize the concept of independent probability. That merely means that two different events that could result in losing or winning do not affect each other. The best example is a coin flip. Flipping a coin results in a 50/50 chance of it coming up heads or tails. Each coin flip does not change the odds of the next coin flip. If the flip results in ten or twenty heads in a row the eleventh or twenty-first flip still has a 50/50 chance of coming up heads again.

If you can wrap your mind around this concept, you can understand that even though you have lost in the past, your past loses are independent of your current attempt. Past loses should be exactly that, past. In the present, you have a fresh coin flip. You have a fresh chance of winning as a result of your efforts with your current attempt regardless of whether you have habitually lost in the past.

Now of course I recognize that much of this depends on whether you have learned from past mistakes. Maybe you do not have the ability, or sufficient resources, or specific intangibles or a formula that could ever win. Those are important things to think about as you analyze your ability to succeed. But, if we are trying to overcome a losing streak or a slump as it is called, then you have to merely make every attempt independent from every other attempt. The point is that when you endeavor to try to win something, do not think about your record. It has nothing to do with the current attempt. Your focus needs to be on the task at hand not whether the coin has come up heads so many times in a row. A losing streak does not have to change the odds of success in your current attempt. They are independent. Let them stay that way.

So let us recap. Losing sucks. Sometimes it happens but that does not mean that it happens every time. Do not ever let it define who you are in business. Do not surrender to always feeling like you will always lose. And finally when you try, really try. That's it.

CHAPTER 29
Getting over Losing the Past

We all do it. The way that we are wired, we cannot help ourselves. Always looking for the grass to be greener on the other side, we sometimes recall a past that was so much better than the present. It always starts the same way. "I remember a time when . . . ." Or, "You know, in the old days, we used to . . ." Or the classic, "In my time, things were much simpler . . . ."

Of course, remembering the past so fondly is usually a byproduct of not being totally honest with ourselves. The present is frustrating and so we harken back to what we want to recall are "better days." Advertisers sometimes talk about reminding us of the "simpler times." Or sometimes they talk about the past as though people had greater values and had a better work ethic or that people in general were of a better quality. There probably were high quality people back then but there were usually a lot of low-lifes who we put out of our collectively memories as well. We remember things that we selectively wish to remember while ignoring some of the less desirable aspects of our life experiences.

For the record, fondly remembering the past is not a bad thing. I do think it is better than always remembering the bad aspects of every situation and person we have met. We all know people who do that. "Oh those times weren't so great and that guy wasn't all that good a person, I remember once when he . . . ." But for the most part, people often get caught up thinking that some things, important thing, were better in the past. I guess sometimes you truly cannot appreciate the fun you had on a carnival ride until it stops.

Sometimes, if we have the requisite wisdom, we do appreciate the times and special moments in life that are passing us as they are passing us. Maybe you felt it as you played catch with your son. Maybe you expressed it out on the golf course when you told the others, "this is as good as it gets." Maybe you felt it when you talked to someone who you had not talked to in a long while. You realized how much you enjoy talking to them while you are talking to them. For those of you who have cherished a moment while it was still happening, you should know that you are truly fortunate. Some people never get that feeling. Some never stop long enough to "smell the roses" as they say. Some will never have the feeling of knowing how wonderful it feels to have someone make them laugh and appreciate the simple act of laughing.

In business, we seldom if ever feel good about our day. Usually, we are so busy making a buck that we forget how much fun it can be to make the buck in the first place. Face it, you never really sit and say, I am really enjoying helping this customer. We never comment to ourselves, this administrative task really has been a wonderful experience.

For the most part, we look backwards with our appreciation for our small businesses. "Boy I remember the day we got that big order . . ." "I remember depositing that check, now that was a check . . ." "I remember that old office, it was drafty and damp, it was dusty and dirty, my desk was a mess and it was cramped, but it was the best office I ever had . . ."

As we spend more time in business, these memories accumulate. We recall the simplicity of those times as opposed to our current challenges. We fool ourselves into thinking that those times were simpler only because whatever the challenge was back then, we overcame it. Now, unsure that we can overcome our current challenges, we believe that the past was "easier."

After a while, we sit in our little businesses lamenting the goods times as they are passing us or have already passed by us. We wish that we could go back in time to those simpler days. We regret that time is passing so quickly. It is an overwhelming feeling. We feel that we are losing the past. Time rushes by and things change so quickly. We get used to something for better or for worse and then time throws us another curve ball. We adapt. We get used to the change and then what happens? Things change again. We cling to something and it becomes obsolete or worse yet, we become isolated with it. Heck, I would continue to use DOS if I could because I learned how to do all the commands. Now I see Windows in its 3000th edition and all I can think is C:\SCREWTHIS.EXE.

The danger this poses to your business is that it distorts your perspective in dealing with the current problems of your business. You begin to resent the present. Resentment becomes avoidance in some cases. Resentment becomes flat out hatred in extreme cases. Nevertheless, you attitude towards your current situation poisons your attitude towards the business. Having a bad attitude towards your business is contagious. Others will catch it from you.

What is worse is that the past looms with your fond memories for comparison. You become frustrated with the present and your memories from the past console you. The fondness for these memories grows and the present become more frustrating. The vicious cycle feeds itself.

Then, a new frustration starts creeping in. You become concerned that things now will never seem as good as they were in the past. Your outlook becomes bleak as you feel that all the best things from the past are slipping away. All the things you liked about your business do not seem present at present. You feel that you are losing something but you cannot put your finger on what. Life in your business becomes confusing, frustrating, overwhelming and potentially, not worth it. Why can't things just be the way that they were?

So how do we get over losing the past?

The first step is rather simple. You need to recognize that you cannot stop time from marching right on by. The nature of your small business is that you cannot stop. You could slow down the pace from time to time, but you cannot stop things. The truth is, business is dynamic. It is moving and it is changing and you must move and adapt. You might not like the changes but you also might not have a choice. So get over it.

The second step is to put the past in perspective. Was it better? Maybe in some ways it was while in other ways, it wasn't. The trick is to not let your feelings about the past affect how you feel about the present. If you want to feel good about the past, go ahead. If you want to remember only the good things about people and situations, then that is a great way to be. People will love you for that. But, if all you do is compare the past to the present, then you will skew your perception. Face it, the past and the present are probably not all that different. So do not compare them.

The third step is to commit to appreciating the passage of time. This one needs an analogy to make it more concrete. Do you recall the time before VCR's. No not Beta. I mean the time before we could rewind television. Do you recall the time before you could hit one button and re-watch what you might have missed. In those days, we had to pay attention more closely because it was not going to be repeated. If you missed it you missed it. If there was something you really enjoyed seeing, you had to focus on that when it was shown because once it was gone, it was gone.

Now think about your experiences in a movie theater. You have to watch intently so as not to miss anything. The projectionist will not rerun something if you happened to not be paying attention.

Let the feeling sink in. Now, apply that feeling to your business. You do not have a button that will let you rewind. If something good happens today you should enjoy it when it happens and move on. If something bad happens, then let it go the minute it passes you by. Do not rewind to catch something that you missed. The time you face in you small business does not rewind. It is moving and it will not pause or rewind. Just like in the theater. If there is a plot change, you have to go with it. You do not have time to think about the other plot because you need to focus on where the movie is going now.

Finally, you need to look to the future with anticipation. For you Type-A personalities that does not mean anxiety. It means just anticipation. The thinking is this: if thinking about today is not appealing and thinking about yesterday only provides more frustration about thinking about today, then thinking about tomorrow could be your best alternative.

Healthy anticipation can recharge your batteries and can get you over the feelings you have about losing the past. Look at the future and wonder if it can be as wonderful as you remember the past being. Whereas fond recollections of the past required memory, anticipation of the future requires imagination. Begin to imagine how things can be. Start to plan for them. Start to appreciate them. And then, use what you know from the past and what you are doing in the present to make them happen.

CHAPTER 30
Getting Over that Not So Fresh Feeling

Until I wrote this, I had no idea what those commercials were about indicating that a woman and her mother were concerned about their "not so fresh feeling" days. Then somebody told me and I was embarrassed. Not for myself mind you but for the advertiser.

So what about that "not so fresh feeling" when it comes to operating your own business? Excuse the analogy but businesses can go through difficult times that are not so different from what I imagine menstruation is like. And let's face it, the pain is real. In all due respect to women, we men cannot imagine what you women imagine that you are going through. But that is because we men have the sensitivity of a rock.

Now that all genders are offended, let us move on. The reason for my rather off-color analogy is that the "not so fresh feeling" is a reflection of how you will sometimes feel about your business much the same way women will feel about their bodies. You might be mad at your business. You might feel that it has not lived up to your expectation in certain situations. You might be disgusted with it for no real reason. Generally, you will have times that you will not be happy and you might be specifically unhappy with your business or outright angry with it. The point is that your business will sometimes leave you in a foul mood.

That not do fresh feeling in your business will come in different ways. Business dry spells may cause that foul mood. Maybe being too busy will cause that foul mood. Perhaps everyday little annoyances will build up and eventually result in bad feelings toward your business. There is no set formula applicable to all businesses as to why you will feel angry or otherwise to your particular business.

Although it might happen monthly, for example, when bills are due, the feeling could come at any time. It might happen more than monthly. What's worse, its duration might not be merely a few days. Heck, I have known women who have suffered from the effects of their period for twenty seven days and then had one good one before repeating the cycle. That condition typically went away on its own after they stopped dating me however.

So now here you are facing the possibility of having these bad feelings toward your business that can pop up at almost anytime and you do not know what to do about them. Well I would not have written about this and I would not have risked so many people finding me to be a vulgar bastard unless I had some ideas for you. Face it, when I use menstruation as an analogy, I am out on a limb. I better make it pay off with some really snappy advice.

So what is the great advice? First of all, do not panic. There is almost always something that can be done about those bad days in your business. If you have to, you can sell it or close. That way, you divorce yourself from your business and you do not have to harbor those bad feeling anymore. If that route seems too drastic or impractical, then you can do other things to overcome those bad feelings.

By the way, when I say impractical, I mean that there will be times when you cannot merely close the doors or sell. Maybe you need the income. Maybe your clients or customers need you. Perhaps there simply is no way for you to stop business without causing some consequences that would adversely affect numerous people. In these instances, you need to take my second piece of advice on the subject of getting over that no so fresh feeling: be creative.

Creativity is probably what led you to open your own business in the first place. Unless you could envision yourself operating your own business, you never would have opened it. Unless you could have seen yourself solving problems and obtaining some level of satisfaction in your own business, you would not have opened the door. If your imagination was sharp enough to see yourself in business before you opened, then you probably have the requisite creativity to face and overcome those not so fresh days.

One creative idea is to change your surroundings. Redo your office. Buy a small piece of furniture. Move some pictures around. Try a new background for your computer desktop. These things can cause you to change your perspective. Overtime, your bad feelings may fade or completely disappear.

Another creative idea is to seek distractions. If possible, seek productive distractions. If your business is getting to you, take a half hour off and play a computer game. That is a distraction. If your business is getting to you, take an hour off and go visit some customers with a box of doughnuts and BS with them for a while. Convince them to send you more business. That is a productive distraction. Any distraction that pays some sort of dividend, no matter how small, is a productive distraction.

Another bit of advice when you face that not so fresh feeling is to get busy. Accomplish a big task and guarantee yourself some reward for accomplishing it. If I finish all the billing in the office by noon on Friday, I will go golfing that afternoon. Here is a radical idea, do something that you have put off out of sheer procrastination. I would bet that getting that out of the way will make you feel infinitely better.

Here is another piece of advice for that not so fresh feeling: give yourself something to look forward to. Schedule a vacation or a special dinner or even just some time away from the office. Give yourself something to hope for in exchange for surviving the bad feelings you have toward the business. It is amazing how good kids can be during the weeks before Christmas while they look for a pay off from Santa Claus. As a result of being preoccupied with what they are looking forward to in the future, they forget the things that are frustrating them in the present.

Another bit of advice is to find someone to bitch to and bond with them. Call a colleague and complain and see if they get the same feelings. Look for a sympathetic ear. Find someone else who has been in your same boat and appreciate the fact that they got out of it and recognize that you can too. Basically, whine, cry and rag. Get the bad feeling out of your system.

The final piece of advice for those not so fresh feelings is to walk away. Notice I did not say abandon. All I said was walk away. Go out to lunch. Go spend time with your kids, Take the dog for a walk. Put someone else in charge and get away for a day or two.

Realize that none of these things will stop those feelings from coming back but, they can make them go away for the time being. By recognizing that you can engage in techniques that will allow you to get past the bad feelings, you can enjoy the good times more. During the times that you have good feelings toward the business, you do not have to obsess over those bad feelings days because you have ideas of what to do to get past them. You will develop ideas on how to get over them. Soon those bad feeling days will become more manageable. They will become more controllable. They will become annoyances rather than problems. They will become minor obstacles rather than obstructions. They will fade in their importance to you.

Perhaps most importantly, by learning how to face those not so fresh feeling days, you will become the person who controls your bad feelings toward your business rather than your bad feelings controlling you. You will strip away a vulnerability and begin to appreciate that having occasional bad feelings toward your business is just another aspect of owning and operating your business. A new perspective will dawn on you. Bad days will become challenges not problems. And as you think about it, if you did not appreciate challenges, then why did you open your own business in the first place?

CHAPTER 31
Getting Over Winning
(Or, Getting Over Yourself)

Now that we have discussed all the sad things that can happen when you have to get over certain things, we now look at that happy circumstance of winning and success. Some of you might have considered skipping this chapter. You might think, why should I work on getting over success? Because, regrettably, for many people, getting over your own success is all about getting over yourself. For those of you who do not have to get over yourself then you need to worry about the other related problem that success can inspire: complacency.

Now I assure you that there is nothing wrong with success. It is in fact what you want no matter how you define it. But, success can present certain problems for certain people who operate their own businesses. There is a small part of the narration in the very end of the movie "Patton" where academy award winner, George C. Scott, relays the story a Roman emperor who is parading through Rome with his captives after a successful campaign. The emperor is wearing a golden crown and the audience is showing its appreciation. And as the story is told, there is a small detail about a slave sitting in the emperor's chariot whispering in the emperor's ear over and over again that "all glory is fleeting."

Well, I am here to tell you, the fact that all glory is fleeting appears indisputable. Look, let's face it, anything that you might have won yesterday does not matter today. I can never understand why this concept appears lost on baseball managers. The never understand that their past success counts for nothing. They always look like a deer caught in the headlights when they are about to get fired. "The team was winning just last week, I don't understand why you are firing me!" Well in business today you have to look at yourself like a baseball manager. You might have been successful two days ago but if you were not successful yesterday and this afternoon, then you are behind. Some managers protest, "but we have a winning record?" And the owner simply nods and says, "but you haven't won lately." Smart managers know that despite past success your most recent record is all that counts. Such a mind set will prevent you from ever getting complacent. You feel the pressure to win everyday.

Meanwhile, some people actually achieve success on a regular basis. How do they get over it? The truth is, some do and some do not. The ones that do seem to have a secret that the ones do not almost never seem to fully comprehend even when they know the secret. Successful people who do not let the success go to their head have humility. And although some successful people know what the word means, they cannot seem to acquire the feeling.

Humility is a pretty warm blanket. It keeps you grounded and safe. It makes you look comfortable to others. Most importantly, it does not let you get exposed. People who bask in their success without humility seem to always get exposed. Fate keeps a watchful eye on those who let success go to their head. Sometimes success leads to overconfidence. Fate somehow knows how to chill overconfidence.

Aside from keeping you warm and protecting you from exposure, humility also keeps you grounded. Humble winners appreciate everything outside of themselves that make them successful. There is nothing more gracious than a winner who thanks everyone else with sincerity for whatever honor is bestowed for the winner's triumph. Often times, recognizing that you were lucky, or if you consistently succeed, that you are lucky, is one of the best ways to remain humble. Whereas fate is conscious of the ungrateful winner, fortune smiles on those who pay tribute to good luck. So thank your lucky stars from time to time. It is a sign of humility and gratitude to those forces that help us even when we do not deserve it.

In order to become humble, you need to experience humility. The way to experience humility with your success is to fully embrace the concept of not thinking about what your success means to you but instead what does it mean for others. This does not mean that you think that others admire you. Thinking that is really only considering what success means to you. When you think about what your success means to others you are thinking in terms of the consequences of your success and the benefits others enjoy from that success. This is the basis of humility in the wake of success.

Think about all the many people who have tirelessly gone on to achieve success that only benefitted others. Think about the work of Louis Pasteur or Mother Theresa. Their efforts and success benefitted the many people who they thought about and cared for. Think of those soldiers who were in every winning battle and each time tried hard to succeed not for themselves but for their country. Think of the lawyer who dedicates his life's work to the service of his clients and acquires a substantial winning record on behalf of many clients who are too poor to pay him. Think about the doctor who tries and is successful at saving so many lives in an emergency room and despite being able to quit and work in a less stressful environment, continues to work where he is needed most. Think of the businessperson who works hard and gets promotions and raises just so that he or she can make a better life for his or her family.

Now think about yourself. If you have achieved success, ask yourself who that success has benefitted. If your goal was to make a lot of money and you acquire wealth from your success, ask yourself what you did with that wealth. More importantly, ask yourself who other than you benefits from that wealth. As you think about it you begin to realize the truth of the situation. People who achieve success with humility are driven to succeed for others and for the benefit of others. They are motivated by succeeding for others. They do not measure their success on the basis of what it means to themselves. They are focused on how they can succeed for others. And, as they succeed time after time for others, their success produces a deeper meaning and is that much more satisfying.

My goodness. You read a chapter or two like this and you begin to think that you are in church listening to a sermon. "Yes Scott, you're right. I should only try to be successful for others. My humility will help me to work for and benefit others. Thank you Scott for the insight." And then you moon me or flip me the bird.

I am not trying to preach to you. I am too cynical to think that you have time for me to preach. My observations are more scientific than spiritual. The observations here are based on human nature. Remember, my point is that some people need help getting over their success. Can you change your, dare I say it, perspective? If you do not think about your success in terms of yourself then you do not have to get over yourself. If your only measure of success is what you can achieve for others than you possess the requisite humility to always get over yourself. Because you are committed to succeeding for others, you really are not likely to get complacent. The complacency that creeps in when you say to yourself, I have accomplished all I need to accomplish for myself is not present when you think about succeeding for others. In thinking about succeeding only for yourself, there is less pressure because you know that you will forgive yourself for not succeeding or perhaps not even trying hard. But, when you try to succeed for others you always feel pressure. You want the success for them not merely for yourself. You live with the pressure that if you do not try your best, someone may be disappointed.

Perhaps most importantly, the satisfaction you feel in succeeding for others is more profound than when you succeed merely for yourself. You are appreciated by more people when you succeed for others. This is somewhat egotistical and therefore should help even the most cynical of you appreciate the meaning. If your success for others makes them appreciate you or even merely like you, then you will feel that much better about yourself. You see. You can be happy now so long as you feel that your success for others has some benefit for yourself.

There is another phenomenon to achieving success for others that I cannot explain in terms of human nature. Somehow when you devote your time and efforts to succeeding for others and solving their problems, your own success and problems seem to take care of themselves. That might be spiritual but I cannot confirm it. I have already offended my cynical readers enough.

CHAPTER 32

Getting Over a Slump, Lay off or Vacation
Or Simply, Getting back on Track, Getting back to Work, Getting back to Business, _____ (fill in additional clichés here)

There will be times in your business when you need to stand back, take stock and refocus. I would caution that it should not happen every day but, there will be times when it is necessary. Some of you might already be thinking that there is lost time and efficiency whenever you need to restart something so why not just keep working. Think about a pull start lawnmower. If you let it stop, then you will have to strain your back and arm restarting it. While this is a valid point, if you do not stop cutting the lawn every once in a while to see what you have already cut and look at how good you are doing, then the job might get sloppy. So it is worth stopping now and then and paying the price to restart a job in order to assure that it is done right.

Some Type A personalities try to schedule the times that they will stop and refocus. They set some arbitrary date or time at which they will stop, look over what they have accomplished, and begin again. I cannot see how that could be effective because the times to stand back and take stock and refocus cannot be arbitrarily set on any particular schedule. Such times to stop and reassess usually needs some sort of precursor. There needs to be some intervening event that will bring you to that point where you need to stand back.

Now sometimes, much like engaging in some athletic exercise, you need to merely catch your breath. In athletic endeavors, catching one's breath usually fulfills more than a physiological need for air. It provides an opportunity to think. It is like pressing th reset button on your brain. It allows you to step away, regain your perspective, and start a little fresher.

In business, as I have already pointed out, this need to reset usually follows some precursor. For different people and for each different business, there are different precursors. For some people, it will come after a short downturn in business. In sports they call it a slump. For others, it may come after either a forced lay-off or a vacation. Many times it follows an over due vacation. For yet others, it might follow some significant event. Such events might include the closing of a major deal or a big sale or the completion of the busy season. No matter what the precursor might be for your particular business, however, the precursor serves a purpose in causing a brief stop or a pause. This is important because in order to effectively refocus, you need a time out to do it.

After the precursor, whatever that might be, you need time to assess what is going on in your business. If the precursor was effective in serving its purpose, the assessment will begin in the wake of greater clarity. Clarity is vital for your assessment of where the business has been, where it is and where it is headed. You need to be able to perform an honest assessment. The more dramatic the precursor, the more wide sweeping the assessment.

Now for all the abstract crap that I have just laid on you, the way to make it concrete is to think about your situation. Imagine how you usually feel the day after you get back from a vacation. All the problems that you had before you left do not seem so bad. All the terrible things that you left behind, as you think about them now, are not so terrible. You may have gained a new perspective on your problems. Maybe you have even gained a new appreciation for the people in your business who help you solve your problems. Perhaps, you have even gained a new appreciation for your business's ability to solve and handle problems.

What caused this epiphany? Sometimes just being away from the business is all you need to put it back in focus. That is what vacations are really all about. Sure a vacation that offers you the opportunity to go to different places and experience new things is important for itself but, to the entrepreneur, it is also an important respite. It allows you to get away from the business and its problems long enough to start to think about everything in a whole new light.

When your vacation is over, you do have some lost efficiency in getting back to business. You have to pull that starter cord again. But, if you had continued without the vacation then it is possible that you would have continued to perform with diminished or virtually no efficiency. Maybe, without stopping, you would have accidentally tailed off in the wrong direction. Maybe, without stopping to reassess, you would have been doing things that were counterproductive and that you would not have done if you had merely stopped to think about it.

Ralph was one of the most intelligent home builders I have known. He had been in the industry for twenty years the last five of which in his own business. He had seen everything and he was very reliable. His experience made him pretty efficient and he knew the people he liked to work with to get jobs done and to keep his very prominent clientele satisfied. He had developed a routine of only working on one home at a time. This routine had served him well until, he met twin sisters who had wanted to build two homes near each other. These two sisters had been as different as night and day but the problems that Ralph would have with the two of them would confirm that they were sisters. An unhealthy competition existed between them and Ralph got caught in the middle.

Ralph had been completing a rather large and complicated job at the time he met the sisters. They had come to him with a plan to build two homes, one for each of them. They had obtained a set of plans from a prominent architect with whom Ralph was familiar. The plans were about seven years old and the sisters expressed that they had commissioned the plans years before but were waiting until they had found the two properties within close proximity to build in order to be near each other. The plans for each home were identical to one another except for a few minor modifications. The two parcels that they had purchased were about two blocks from one another in the same neighborhood. It seemed easy enough. Ralph had considered that because he would be working off the same plans and because the projects were so close to one another, there would be many potential opportunities to save money and be more efficient than if it were merely two completely separate jobs. He could take advantage of production schedules and deliveries in order to make the jobs very profitable. He also learned that the two sisters had plenty of money and were willing to spend heavily on add-ons. Ralph had thought that the endless supply of cash from his clients would be a blessing. He would find that he was mistaken however.

So Ralph commenced work on the two homes immediately after he was finished with one of the bigger jobs he had been doing that year. A break would have served him well but he wanted to move onto these two new projects. The clients were anxious to get started as well. Ralph was confident. There is an old saying. "Man plans, God laughs." Ralph was the man.

As I had said, Ralph knew the architect but he had not actually spoken to him before taking the job. It seemed he had retired in the years since he had drawn up these plans. Ralph tried but he could not reach him. He could not even find him. So Ralph brought in his own people to work on the project and took on a new consulting architect to help get the two jobs done. At first, things had gone well but Ralph soon learned that the sisters each had some very distinct demands for their respective homes. Ralph tried to be accommodating but the sisters were relentless. As each saw something that the other had done, each sought to modify her own plans to "one up" her sister. The respective projects were spinning out of control as each sister would strive to push for changes that would take each project in completely different directions. At one point, these constant modifications began taking their toll on Ralph as he tried to smile through each set of changes. Despite his best efforts to remain calm, however, things began to unravel.

After a few weeks, Ralph learned that the sisters had been responsible for driving the original architect to an early retirement through their constant desire to compete with one another. He had retired on the verge of being driven insane by the two sisters. The constant changes that each was putting on Ralph's projects caused delays and soon both projects fell behind. Each sister, unbeknownst to the other, began to offer Ralph bribes to abandon the other sister's project and complete their own. The two would always be pleasant to one another but in private, they would stab each other in the back.

Soon, the minor catastrophes encountered in each job lead to full scale disaster for Ralph. As things fell behind, the contractors began to get upset. The sisters would try to bribe the contractors and were interfering with the work site on a daily basis. Before too long, Ralph had completely lost control. It was the day that one sister asked if her basement could be converted to an in ground swimming pool that Ralph became unhinged. He politely explained that it could not and he walked out of the office. He got into his truck and tried to determine where the nearest cliff was. He had had enough. He felt that he could not go on. Just then, his phone rang, it was the other sister wondering how much more it would cost to convert the attached garage from a two car to a four car.

Two of Ralph's contractors found him severely pounding his head against the steering wheel of his truck. He had snapped. The two projects were so out of control that it seemed impossible for him to get the job done. The two sisters had been so demanding that he really did not care anymore. His nerves were shot. He could not go on. Anything he did at that juncture was useless.

He was in my office the following Friday morning asking what his liability would be for quitting in the middle of the projects. He was scared to go back. During our consultation, each sister had called him twice with completely different questions each time. I felt so bad for him. I advised him of the legal ramifications of stopping and that did not make him happy. He asked me if I knew where the nearest cliff was. Realizing that his problems were not legal, I gave him some advice that, believe it or not, helped.

The first thing he did was turn off his phone. Second, we jumped online and booked him a quick flight to Las Vegas. We got him a room on the strip and we got him a flight leaving in two hours. He was scheduled to return in two days. Ralph swore that he could not leave even as I escorted him onto the plane. I took his cell phone away and saw his flight take off.

What happened next was magical. When Ralph returned that Monday, he seemed like a new man. He had a new focus. The first thing he did was call a meeting with his contractors and he discussed what could be done for both worksites to make things more efficient. Everyone agreed that having the sisters kept off premises would help. Then, Ralph reworked out production schedules considering what progress had been done on each job. He moved materials from one job to the other in order to create more efficiency at both sites. Essentially, he did what he had originally envisioned when he agreed to do both jobs simultaneously. He had originally planned to take advantage of certain things in the respective production schedules to make the two jobs more efficient. But, having been bogged down in the sisters' constant intervening, he had lost focus. That plan had been lost. But, he was back to his original plan.

He also did something else that seemed brilliant. It was not my idea so I feel comfortable saying it was brilliant. He casually told one of the sisters about how some of his most prominent clients usually never stay to watch the final phase of construction. He told her about how all the "big shots" usually go out of town for the final phase after giving one final set of instructions. He told her that it was a typical practice of the more affluent people with whom he had done business. He told her that these wealthy types would figure that going away before the final phase of construction would be the last vacation that they would take for a while because once they got back, they would spend all their time getting acclimated to the new house. The sister smiled as she took in what Ralph had said. She made a point of telling Ralph that she had already scheduled a trip to Europe during the final phase just as some of her more wealthy acquaintances always did. She made it seem as though she was aware of the practice. When Ralph relayed the same information to her sister, she let him know that she would be going to the Far East and that he was to make an off handed mention of that fact to her sister.

   With both sisters out of town, the contractors were all too happy to quickly get the job done. Ralph had pulled it together and he had overcome something that had brought him to the brink of quitting. To this day, Ralph never told me what happened in Vegas because I guess what happens there stays there. It seems to be a Nevada statute or something. But, just the same, that trip worked. Ralph got back on track and back to completing a job he did not think he could. He had turned things around and found new and creative ways to solve his problems. He regained control.

   That is what a good break or a distraction can do for you. It might offer you insight as to how to solve your problems. It might give you some new and creative ways of approaching the problems. It might merely help you to refocus on what your original plan was and it might help you to get back to it. In all, in trying to get over a slump or getting back on track, a break or distraction can help to let you regain perspective. There is that word again.

PART V
Those Big Decisions

CHAPTER 33
Decision-Making for the Entrepreneur:
Just How Much Information do You Need Anyway?

Maybe you have heard the old sayings and adages mentioned in this book. Most of them are things that I have heard time and time again over the years. Most, if not all of them have been uttered by small business owners who, in the attempt to understand their circumstances, refer to these sayings for a small bit of relief or even comfort. Somehow by recalling these various adages they recognize that others must have faced the situations that they are facing and that those others must have made it through. Then the small business owner feels that if someone else faced this situation and they overcame it successfully, then there is at least a chance that the small business owner can get passed the situation as well.

To better illustrate this phenomenon, I rely upon the following analogy. If you feel like you are a mouse in a maze and you fear that there is no way out, then watch to see if any other mouse has made it through the maze. If you know for certain that other mice have made it through the exact same maze, then you can continue on knowing that whatever you are trying to accomplish can be accomplished. This is no guarantee of success however. Or, more accurately, this is no guarantee of your success in your given situation. But, at least you know that what you are attempting to accomplish is not impossible. Small business owners find relief and comfort in that knowledge. Their feeling is always the same: it might be difficult but, at least we know it can be done.

So what has all of this to do with decision making? After all, the lead under the chapter heading mentions that this chapter will be about decision making. Please note that this is why I make the lead-ins under the chapter headings humorous and/or ironic or at least somewhat interesting. It makes the reader inclined to read them.

185

So, good for you. You read the lead-in and I am glad. Yes indeed. This chapter is about decision-making. And, as you might expect, I am going to rely upon an old adage to help try to explain what entrepreneurs do when faced with important decisions.

Let's face it. If you have a major decision to make, then you are at what is often referred to at a "crossroads." You could go down one path or another or maybe several others. Having to make an important decision is stressful. You want to make sure that you make the right choice. The stress is the result of how different people make decisions.

It is a good thing to be decisive. That description of people is highly coveted in the business context. "She's a decisive manager." That means that she has a reputation for making a decision and not avoiding it. And it means that once she makes a decision, she does not try to go backwards. She makes decisions without regret and she commits to the decisions she makes be they good or bad. She tries to make good ones but does not obsess over trying to fix the bad ones.

Some people, (for example: women) always regret their past decisions. The minute that they are not happy with a decision that they have made, and the very second that they realize that they cannot change their minds and choose another path, then they regret the decision that they have made. For them, the grass is always greener at the house they should have chosen. Over time, these types of people undermine themselves in all decision-making situations. They have no confidence in themselves to make right decisions because they always feel that they have made the wrong decisions. For you husbands out there think about your wives. Almost all wives have memories of the other guy who they could have dated and eventually married rather than you. Somehow these perfect guys never seemed to get around to asking your wife to marry them but that was certainly not your wife's fault. As your wife thinks about this guy, she begins to regret her decision to marry you. She does not resent you per se but she has some regret. Sure the other guy eventually became a homicidal maniac, but, as your wife sees it, unlike you, at least he picked up after himself. So being a simple minded husband you ask your wife, "would you be happier with me if I was more conscientious about picking up after myself even if I killed a bunch of people like the guy you feel that you should have married?" And your dear wife, without missing a beat, will hold up the newspaper that has the other guy's mug shot and a story about his conviction and she will say to you, "don't be silly, he's also better looking than you."

Then there is the other type of decision-maker. Let's call them . . . . oh, I don't know . . . guys. Guys never regret the decisions that they did not make. They never think about the path that they should have chosen. For them, what is passed is passed. You cannot go back so do not obsess over it. For guys the important thing to think about is how do we fix the decision that we have made already. They do almost no planning about future decisions. At least, with a little regret, they might think more before making their next decision. Maybe they will not have to waste time trying to fix every decision that they have made if they took more time in making their past decisions. The problem for them is that guys do not see themselves as poor decision makers. They just make decisions and for better or worse, they live with the consequences.

To these poor schlubs you ask the question, "so the wife you chose let herself go and became real bitchy. What would have happened if you had married that other girl you were dating?"

And poor schlub has a stupid look on his face, "which girl?"

And you respond, "you know, the other one you dated before you met your wife."

And then finally a light bulb goes on. He responds, "oh yeah, her, I forgot about her."

And you, feeling as if you are talking to a brick, ask him, "aren't you curious about what ever happened to her? Maybe she didn't let herself go. Maybe she's not so pissy like your wife. Don't you ever wonder what happened to her?"

And poor schlub looks at you and says, "oh yeah, I know what happened to her. My wife showed me this story in the paper. She married some homicidal maniac. From what I understand, the guy always picked up after himself though."

So what is the point of all of this? Well, that is where the adage I rely upon comes in. This old adage along with my modification of it goes to the heart of the two types of decisions makers' problem. Their problem is based on information. Not what specific information is necessary but instead the quantity of information that various types of people use to make

187

decisions.

The adage goes like this:

"Fools rush in where Angels fear to tread."

Hopefully you have heard it. Now for my addition to it.

"Fools rush in where Angels fear to tread. But, if someone must go in, then thank God for fools."

From what we have discussed thus far, let's consider women to be Angels and guys to be fools. If we do that, then maybe I will not be seen as so offensive for what I said about women and regret. Meanwhile I called guys "schlubs" and, the poor fools either do not know or have already forgotten that I offended them.

Anyway, this adage, with my addition, addresses the issue of decision making for small businesses. It is worth repeating: *"Fools rush in where Angels fear to tread. But, if someone must go in, then thank God for fools."*

For our purposes, we can draw the inferences out of it and look at what it implies.

We start with: *"Fools rush in."* That means that people without enough information make decisions. They are fools because they do not have all the information necessary to make the decision. They are relying upon luck to help them with the decision. "Rushing in" implies that the fool is being hasty in making the decision.

Back to our discussion about husbands. I know guys who took less time getting to know their eventual wives than they did picking a shaving cream. Guys would pick wives out of a catalogue that showed only a picture and statistics if you let them. "How big are her breasts? Oh, she'll do."

The point is that good decision making should not be done hastily or without considering at least some information.

Back to the adage. *"Where Angels fear to tread."* This implies that making a decision can be avoided. Angels do not like finality of decisions. Angels do not buy dresses that they cannot return for six months after

188

purchase if they later decide that they do not like them.   Angels, like women, have drawers full of receipts for the option to return every thing that they *decided* to buy. The wife comes home with a new dress. She asks her husband his opinion. "Here it is honey. This is the dress I decided to buy. What do you think?" Most women do not understand that we would rather see them naked and we really do not care what they are wearing but we small minded guys play along. "It's nice Honey."

But, any guy with a spine really should respond like this, "Well Honey let's see. Have you cut the tags off?" She answers, "no of course not." Mr. Spine asks, "do you have your receipt?" She answers with growing frustration "of course I do." He asks, "and you could change your mind and take it back right?" Becoming angry she replies, "yes." He then says with conviction, "then you didn't 'decide' to buy it did you? I mean, really, because you could take it back you have yet to decide whether you have bought it. You see, you really haven't 'decided' at all."   In this scenario, Mr. Spine is right. He is going to be very lonely but he is right.

The point is that if you can still change your mind and go down another path without consequences, you have not yet made a decision. Decision should imply final.

So Angels will not tread where they have to make a final decision and where they cannot go back. Not being able to go back, or change their minds, that is what angels fear.   Angels need to be sure what is going to happen next. They want what I call "no liability" decision making. They want to be able to make decisions that are based on all information available including a precise forecast of the future so that no one can blame them for a bad decision. The do not want to be responsible for the consequences of a bad decision.

Think about your wife again. She is almost never responsible for any bad decisions. Why not? Because she ran every decision past you and you approved the bad ones. "We bought a house with a leaky roof," you tell her. She responds, 'you said to buy it." "You told me that you liked this dress," She tells you, "and so I didn't take it back." You of course have never told her that any dress looks bad on her but, to her, that is not the point. So you say, "So?" And she replies, "well I wore it to that party last week and not one of my friends has called me to tell me how great I looked so I must have looked like hell, thanks a lot, once again you made a disastrous decision that cost me." Do not shake your head because she is serious. The truth is that wives pawn off the bad decisions that they might have made on their idiot husbands. It is amazing. Your youngest child gets in trouble at school and your wife tells you, "well you wanted one more child." Your oldest of seven gets into trouble at school and she says, "you know I never said that I wanted children. That was your decision."

Now men may ask, my wife did make the decision to marry me when I proposed right? As she so often points out, that was a bad decision. Actually, men only think that it was their decision to propose. Any woman who immediately accepts a proposal of marriage had decided to marry the guy long before he got the idea to marry her. Where did the idea to marry her come from? She put it there when he was not looking. Face it, if she said "yes" right away, then you were manipulated my friend. Do not feel bad, it happens to a lot of guys. She decided that she wanted you to propose and just as she planned, you did. Was her decision to make you propose a bad one? Well I have yet to meet a wife who is as happy as she feels she could be, but most look at the decisions to marry who they marry as a temporary lapse of judgment. It is only a small blemish on an otherwise spotless record of decision making. And how did they end up with a spotless record? They married a husband who made all the bad decisions or who approved any poor decisions that the wives made and therefore, the wives were not responsible for any bad decisions after they married their husband. Basically, wives marry into "bad decisions cover."

Moving away from the blame game however, there is a problem faced by people who hesitate to make decisions where they have no one to blame if things go wrong. These people who are often times women want the answer to this question before making any decision: "What will be each and every future consequence of me making this particular decision?" Unable to see the future, they then rely upon obtaining as much information as they can before making any decision.

As I said, guys would select a wife out of a catalogue if they could. Meanwhile, there are women who cannot have enough information about their future husbands. That's why women really do not date as much as they interview prospective husbands. Women look at prospective husbands in an employer-employee sort of manner. If they could, they would ask us for resumes and references. Guys could imagine showing them and discussing our dating history as if interviewing for a job? "Well, I dated Amy for about two years where I learned a lot before moving on to Bonnie where I also learned a lot including heavy sensitivity training . . ." We would have to let them call old girlfriends to ask them what it was like to be with us. "He said that while with you, he learned about how to get along with your parents, is that true?" They would have us guys serve probationary periods in our marriages before letting us poor guys qualify for full benefits. They would reserve the right to terminate us for insubordination.

Then after having all of this information, women would still be willing to go to the Oracle at Delphi to find out how the marriage will ultimately turn out. Being confident that they can, they know that they can remold you into what they want you to be as their husband. But, just in case we are a lost cause, they can never be totally sure. They evaluate us like a carpenter looks at a 2 by 4. We might not look warped at the lumber yard but that is not to say that we will not become warped on the job.

Trying to get too much information can be a delay tactic to avoid making a decision. I could go so far as to say that, in most cases, it is a delay tactic. People who hesitate to make decisions always hope that something will either happen so that the decision does not have to be made or that more information will become available so that they can be sure of their decision. Some people go to the race track with the exact same fifty dollar bill that they had when they came in because they could not be sure that they would pick a winner. So, over time, they decided that they wanted to break even and the only sure way to do that was not to pick any horses and not bet. Meanwhile, others stand at the betting window wishing that eight of the nine horses in the race will get scratched before post time. They then pick the one horse remaining.

Do not misunderstand. Some decision-makers reap the benefit of a delay. Some decisions should be delayed at least until you get more information. But, the acquisition of additional information is a luxury option not available on some decision models. As frustrating as it may seem, some decisions have to be made on gut instinct without additional information.

The Decision you Have to Make Now Scenario:

There is a common scenario of a great applicant who you think might work out for your company. You have interviewed him or her and you are fairly sure it will work out. While you are deciding however, the applicant calls you to let you know that although he or she would like to work for you, another offer has surfaced from one of your competitors. The applicant tells you that they promised to give your competitor an answer by the end of the day.

Your hand is now forced. You do not have any more time. You cannot acquire any more information. You now have to ask yourself, do I trust myself to make this decision?

Sadly, that is the wrong question to ask. Your ability to trust yourself is another distraction. You do not have a choice as to whether to trust yourself. You have to choose. This had to happen because you are in business for yourself. You had to know that at some point you would have to make a decision. So here you are. That day has arrived. Pick! Your confidence in your decision making is of no consequence at this point. You should have thought about that before opening the business. Your ability to trust yourself has been resolved. About that, you have no choice. You must trust yourself because you have to make a decision.

So now, the only question you need to ask is, do you want him or her or not? Tell him or her that you will get back to him or her within the hour. Hang up, pull out a piece of paper, write down and assess the pros and cons of this individual and make the decision.

What else can you do during that hour? Write down your decision and place it in your desk. Then, consult with someone you trust. See if they come to the same conclusion. If they do, feel good. If they do not, listen to why they came to a different conclusion and then do what you intended otherwise. Unless, they considered something you did not in which case, maybe you should reassess. Now look at the clock and see how much of that hour is left. With fifteen minutes left, think about how you feel about your last conversation with the applicant. Do you feel as if you are being held up? Did he or she seem sincere about wanting to work for you? Is he or she forcing your hand? Will this applicant, as an employee, try to force your hand in the future when they want a raise etc.?

There is still ten minutes left. Do you know what I would do? I would call the competitor to see if the applicant really was really being considered. Without giving anything away, I would call the competitor and congratulate them for getting the applicant you interviewed. See how they react. If they react somewhat cocky, tell them about your conversation with the applicant. Tell them that they were the applicant's second choice but that you will let your competitor have him or her. Then tell them why you are willing to lose them. Mention a few pros but detail the list of the cons you write down. I would then call the applicant three hours later to see if they still wanted the job on my terms. I might lose the applicant but, at least I did not get manipulated. The other possibility is that I might get the applicant with some humility instilled. That might make for a good start to the employer-employee relationship.

Now some of you might think: I could never do that. Well, in truth, I probably could not do that to the applicant either. It might be disrespectful to the applicant and to your competitor. In a situation like that, I probably would react differently to the applicant's phone call. I would probably let the applicant know that I had decided to make the decision at the time I had selected to make the decision, for example, the end of the week. I always suggest that you tell any potential applicant the time period in which you will be making the decision at the applicant's interview.

Then, I would let the applicant know that if the other opportunity was there for them, they should take it as I cannot be compelled to make a decision until the time I had said that I would make it. I would tell then that I did not want to stand in the way of another opportunity being available for them. Essentially, I would let the applicant know that the decision to take the other job or not before the end of the day was theirs to make not mine to make for them. I would not say that of course. If the applicant is somewhat sharp, they should realize that is the gist of what I am conveying, however. The point to my decision-making in this scenario is that the applicant's phone call became the major con that could not be overcome. That phone call implies to me that the applicant is looking for information from me to make a decision and that he or she needs my decision within a time frame that I did not dictate.

The point for you is to realize that my decision might be wrong. My reason for making the decision might be wrong. My formula for making the decision might be wrong. If so, then so be it. I made a decision to lose the applicant. Maybe that will eventually prove to be good or bad. The point is that the decision is now over as a result of an unpleasant phone call. Maybe you would have reacted to the phone call differently. Maybe you would be wrong to hire the applicant on the spot. Whatever the reasons for making a decision, once the decision is made, the reasons no longer matter. All you can do is trust yourself and decide.

That is what being in business and making decisions is all about. There is no set formula. There is no right way or wrong way to make a decision. Develop the confidence to make decisions. Learn from bad ones and thank your lucky stars for the good ones.

Chapter 34
Picking Partners versus Picky Partners

This chapter is about maintaining relationships. The specific relationships dealt with are the ones concerning the people who are in business with you. The decisions that you make concerning who you go into business with are long gone. Staying in business with them or removing yourself from the relationship might not be practical. So what decision is there to make? You need to decide what relationship you will have with your partners and fellow shareholders. Some of you may think that there is no way that this is a big decision. You never gave it any thought before so how could it be a big decision. Trust me. It is a big decision. If you do not handle this particular decision well, you will endure considerable and unnecessary suffering.

The decision comes down to: what do you want to be to your partners and what do you want them to be to you. The factors that have a bearing on this decision are all over the spectrum. Do you count on your partners for guidance or expertise in some manner? Do they count on you for cash contributions? Do you need their personality to balance certain aspects of your personality? Do they have to rely upon your creativity while you rely upon their pragmatism?

You also need to think about your relationship with your fellow entrepreneurs visa vie your employees. Remember, employees are like kids. They gravitate towards the easier parent, or in this case partner. Are you a friend to your employees while your partner is their enemy. That leads to bad stuff. You get used and your partner gets abused in these situations.

Are you going to be the fierce money man? Heartless and cruel but profitable.

Do you want to play good cop - bad cop?

Sometimes you have timid partners. They are shrinking violets who fail to assert themselves to you. This leads to significant problems unless you are inherently perfect. For those of you who are fallible however, the failure to have partners assert themselves when you are wrong results in regret and frustration to those who are left to have faith in you.

The decisions concerning your relationships with your fellow partners are dynamic as well. They change over time as you and your partner's needs change. For example, your partner may encounter increased pressure to bring home the bacon if they marry or begin to have a family. A partner who could pocket uncashed paychecks in order to reinvest in the business may not be able to do that once his or her personal situation changes. Was your partner's ability to reinvest at various times when cash flow was bad the only advantage to having him or her as a partner? Perhaps a partner will change as his or her financial rather than mere personal needs change. If your partner is getting older, does he or she spend less time working at the office and planning for his or her retirement? Does your partner suffer health problems or a crisis that removes them from a day to day contribution to the business? Could your partner merely become board with the business and think about investing his or her time and money elsewhere? Does your partner have a personality conflict that develops with you or your other partners that results in the entire situation becoming unworkable? Partners are people whose situations and feelings can change. You need to consider that.

Deciding who should and who should not be your partners in business is probably one of the most critical decisions you can make in your business. Choosing poorly can have dire consequences. There is a saying that a business is only as good as the worst of its operators. Others refer to it as the "weakest link" syndrome. Simply stated, your business will be limited by the least of your partner's ability to manage it. If you choose someone who is lazy, the business will suffer from being seen as lazy to the people who deal with that partner. If you choose someone who is unreliable, the business will be seen as unreliable as well by those people dealing with the unreliable partner. If you choose someone who is untrustworthy, the business will fail regardless of what people think about that partner because you will see the business as untrustworthy as a result of having that type of partner. It is hard to stress enough how important this particular decision is. In so many ways, you hitch your wagon to your partner. You must continually hope that once you do, he or she is going to help you move your wagon and not let it remain stuck in the mud.

One of the best things you can do for your business is to look for partners who have temperament, experience and skill that differs from your

196

own. This will allow the business to be more broad in terms of management. Broad management leads to flexible management. Broad management means that you have the ability to adapt and accommodate more types of people and situations. Broad management means that your business can have different relationships and varying degrees of personal involvement with the individuals you encounter in doing business. Broad management means that the business has a greater wealth of knowledge and experience to draw upon in dealing with others and various situations.

On the other hand, when you are different from your partners, there is a greater likelihood for conflict. Your differences affect how you interact with your partners. Your interest and priorities may be at odds with theirs from time to time. We will discuss the resolution of disputes later in the chapter but for now you need to realize that in choosing a partner who is different from you, the business can benefit despite the fact that your differences make your partnership stressful. Unpleasant partnerships are usually overcome by wealthy or prosperous partners. You might not care for your partner, but if you are making money with him or her, you might not care about your partner either. My God I sound like a fortune cookie writer.

Sometimes, it happens that you do not actually choose your partner. Sometimes these relationships just happen. When they do, these relationships are about as successful as arranged marriages. They depend heavily on luck for the parties to be happy with each other. You cannot depend on that much luck. There are a great many situations in which these relationships happen however.

Perhaps you had a partner who you chose to open the business with many years ago. Then unexpectedly he or she died and their spouse, child, or children inherit the shares of your partner in the business. These are not people you chose yet now you find yourself in business with them by default. In a few cases, you are pleasantly surprised. In all too many cases, it marks the end of the business. Ending the business in these situations does not have to be that tragic. The loss of your partner is tragic. If as a result you need to sell or end the business because of that loss then so be it. You tied your business to a finite life just as your partner did. When one partner dies, that partnership ends. Continuing the business in the wake of losing a partner and forming a partnership with someone whom you did not choose could lead to greater tragedy. You had expectations of your late partner that his heirs may not be able to live up to. This creates a bad situation for you and for them. The alternative is to accept that your partnership had an expiration date. When a partner dies, that is the end. Keeping it going with someone else is like drinking milk after it has expired. Maybe nothing will happen but maybe you will get sick. The truth is, why risk it? Partnerships should always be by choice rather than by happenstance.

There are other situations in which partnerships just happen. These are not the best of circumstances for the business or for you as an operator of a business. You should have a choice in who you decide to operate a business with and your partner should have the same choice. This mutuality makes partnerships largely the result of voluntary associations. Along those same lines, when partners change over time, you should recognize that you might find that you are no longer partners with the person with whom you started the business. If they changed then, as in the case of becoming a partner with your partner's heirs, you might want to choose to end the business. If your partner is not the same then the disputes that might arise may not be able to be resolved readily enough to be able to operate the business smoothly. The important point is that it is the voluntary aspect of the association that should always render your partnership decision to open or close a business as a choice that either partner can make at any time. We do not marry our partners we merely operate businesses with them. When it is no longer in our interest to do so then we have the power to make a decision to terminate the partnership. There is no need for counseling, you can skip right to the divorce. If you do not want to continue as someone's partner you do not have to worry about whether the business is suffering. You can be sure that it is suffering and you can only stop the suffering by discontinuing the partnership.

Of course, the practicality of deciding to end the partnership might have some obstacles. There might be restrictive covenants and other barriers to your departure from the partnership. You should remember that these things are not barriers to your ability to decide to end the partnership. They are barriers to what you can do after you have decided to end the partnership. There is a difference. You can end a partnership and accept the consequences of doing so. Just because there are consequences does not mean that you do not have a choice.

You should also recognize that the decision to end a partnership is the most drastic form of dispute resolution for a partnership. It is not the only manner of resolving disputes but it is the most dramatic. If a partnership reaches an impasse where compromise is no longer possible, ending the partnership may be the only way to resolve the dispute. If one party or the other must get his or her way then all the counseling in the world cannot prevent the inevitable demise of the partnership. At any point where either or any partner puts his or her need to get his or her way before the need to be a partner, then the partnership is over. Being a partner almost by definition means that you do not always get your way. If you cannot accept not getting your way, then you cannot function as a partner. In order to be a partner, the partnership must mean more to you than always getting your way.

Resolving disputes with your partners, short of dissolving the partnership, is perhaps the most difficult thing you will do in business. Because it can be difficult, it should be on your mind when deciding with whom you want to be a partner. If you anticipate that everything you do in business will result in you fighting with your prospective partner then you need to consider that before becoming a partner with him or her. You do not necessarily have to decline to be a partner because you think that there will be disputes or because resolving them will be tough. You merely need to consider that disputes will need to be resolved when you choose your partner in the first place. If you feel the person you are choosing is someone with whom you can settle your differences, then you should still consider being his or her partner.

There are other things to consider in choosing a partner other than merely assessing the likelihood that you will be fighting with him or her. Frankly, there are many other factors to consider only some of which anyone could list because there are so many personal issues for each individual. But, for all of these factors to consider, you should have only one controlling factor to determine whether you can or should be a partner with someone. That one factor has the capacity to render all other factors meaningless if it is not sufficiently resolved.

Some people make a comparison between business partnerships and marriage. Some feel that there are certain analogies. I would disagree. The differences significantly outweigh the similarities. A spouse is someone you choose to live, fight and lose money with. A business partner is someone with whom you choose to work together to make money. Your commitment to your spouse should transcend mere ephemeral relationships and should have a cosmic or spiritual aspect to it. Your commitment to your partners should be based solely upon sound business judgment. Tina Turner may ask, "What's love got to do with it, got to do with it?" Well, if it is her marriage to Ike, then "it" should have to do with love. If "it" is her musical career, then love has nothing to do with her dropping Ike like a bad habit and succeeding on her own. That was sound business judgment. Can spouses be business partners? See Chapter 19.

The point is that there are differences between your marriage and your business partnerships. In deciding who to choose as your business partner you should focus on fewer aspects of the relationship. The considerations for marriage are more numerous. Love, feelings towards children, goals, religion, sex, companionship and compatibility are some of the many considerations for you to choose a spouse. In choosing a business partner, you may have many considerations but your primary consideration should be money. Can you make money with this person? Can you make a living with this person? Other consideration might be important, but the money thing is of primary concern. Some would say that in choosing a spouse you should also consider money. It certainly does not hurt but it should not be the only consideration. In choosing a partner, however, money can be your only consideration.

If the primary consideration in choosing a partner is money then your expectations for one another are severely limited. This can be a good thing. There is a simple standard for you to evaluate the partnership. In marriage, you have many standards to consider and weigh against each other. Is he sensitive to my needs? Is he good to the kids? Is he willing to discuss the relationship? In business, so long as you are making money, you never have to consider the relationship. Nothing else is really important. The questions are easier to answer.

Partner 1, "How do you feel about me as a partner?"

Partner 2, "Well, we made a boat load of cash last month so I would say, you're a damn good one."

Partner 1, "but do you feel that I am sensitive to your needs?"

Partner 2, with a laugh, "You are sensitive to my need for money and I appreciate that."

As you can see, there really is no reason to get caught up in the partnership relationship assessment because all you need to answer for yourself is am I making money with this person.

Having only one primary factor to consider in evaluating a partner eases the decision-making process on your part when you consider certain partners. Are you or can you be friends with a prospective partner? You should not care because it is all about money. "Is he or she a good person?" Once again, who cares? You are partners to make money. "Does he treat his relatives nicely?" If you are making money, and he is not bringing them in to employ them, then why should you care about his relatives? Maybe he treats them like crap and maybe they are crappy to him. If so, who cares so long as your partner can benefit your bank account. Screw his family. For all you know they are a bunch of jerks. Your only concern is can my partner help me to turn a profit and make a living. Because there is only one primary consideration to choosing a partner, partners are easier to choose than spouses.

So now you say, but what about a partner who makes me miserable, should I stay with that partner even if the business is making money? Well, if you are in business solely to maintain friendships then this is a consideration. I am unaware of any real entrepreneurs who have so much cash that they open businesses merely for the sake of having relationships with people but perhaps my experience is limited to those encountered only in reality. Face it. If your partner makes you uncomfortable then chances are, the business is suffering financially from you being miserable. If you are unhappy, somehow that usually gets reflected in the bottom line. In this way, your personal satisfaction with your partner does come into play. But, for it to be a consideration, it should only be important if it affects the bottom line. Otherwise, put your feeling aside and resolve yourself to the concept that operating your own business with a partner is about making money and not about being comfortable or having fun. You are working for each other as partners and you have the obligation to make money together regardless of personal feelings.

So long as you can appreciate that choosing a partner is a big decision, you are likely to take it seriously. When you peel away all the factors for consideration in the selection process, it all comes down to money. Can this partner and I make money together? This is indicative of the type of cold hearted, straight forward decision making that entrepreneurs need to do. Sure, many entrepreneurs wish that they could be more kind or courteous in dealing with their partners. Some of you want to be buddies with your partner. If your are friends, then so be it. As is so often the case, friends do not seem to be able to make money together. You are in business for yourself. You do not need a friend, you need someone with whom to make money. And if you make lots of money, you can buy lots of "friends."

Chapter 35
Should I stay or Should I Go.

The Clash wrote: "if I go there will be troubllllllllle, if I stay there will be doublllllllle . . ." So how about it? Should you stay or should you go? Do you want to stay in business or quit? How do you make that decision?

As with all things in this book, I have no set formula for you. But, I can list the things you might want to consider. Basically, I can give you some, if not most, of the numbers for the formula but I cannot tell you what mathematical signs and symbols to put between the numbers. You can select the signs to put between the numbers to make your own formula. You can put plus signs where you think that they should go and you can put minuses where you think that they should go to decide if you should keep going or stop. Maybe you need to put a multiplication sign in front of certain factors to emphasize them. For example, your retirement should be a factor to consider and, if you are over fifty, you might want to multiply that factor times two or three.

My list of factors to consider is not exhaustive. There are numerous other factors that might be tailored to any one person's individual circumstances. But for the most part, I can provide a list of factors that might result in any individual considering things that they might not have thought about before. After considering all the factors, then you can develop your own formula and possibly include other factors in determining whether you should stay in your own business or pull in your shingle.

Some the factors in making the decision to stay in business seem pretty obvious. Unfortunately, they are not obvious to everybody. Some deal strictly with practical aspects of staying in business while others deal with shear emotional issues. Both types of issues are important. Some people do not think so however. The practical factors like "are you making any money" are easy to assess. For that reason, they are easy to consider. But you should not hesitate to factor emotions into the decision. Emotions play a big part of why you do what you do. In some cases, emotions got you into business on your own. You cannot disregard them. Thinking about how you feel about staying the course or quitting is a big part of the decision.

Some factors are hybrids of practical and emotional factors to consider. For example, you need to consider "what would I do if I quit?" From a practical stand point, this question implies "how would I feed myself?" From an emotional perspective, this question implies "how would I feel about being a quitter and will I take a job with nothing but regret and will I ever feel in control again?" Ask this question: "would I kill myself?" If you did, then you would not have to worry about feeding yourself.

Anyway, here is the list of factors to consider: money, retirement, industry growth, market share of your business, the current and future state of competition, industry projections, personal satisfaction, potential for continuing and future profitability, your own sense of interest in the industry, opportunity, technology, labor and the ability to have others maintain your business, costs and economics, your own ability to handle frustration, futility and accomplishment, Santana, your health and well being, alternatives, your own personal feelings of self worth, availability of talent to assist in the operation of the business, sales forecasts, trends in the industry, availability of necessary supplies and materials, need for investment and additional capital, management, liabilities and the need for legal assistance, insolvency, co-workers and partners, gratification.

I know what I hope that you are thinking. What is Santana? Santana is a rock group lead by legendary Latino guitar player Carlos Santana. I stuck it in there to make sure that you read the whole list. The reason for that is because the whole list is important. If you read each thing on that list you will begin to notice something. You have your own personal additions to that list. There are factors I might not have listed that you want to consider as well. That is why you should read the whole list. The items on my list will give you ideas as to items that should be on your list. I told you that the point of this book and my discussions is to open your mind and not tell you what to think or do. That is what we are doing here. If my list of factors to consider in deciding whether you should stay in business, or not, causes you to think of things to be added to the list, then this book has done its job.

So now that you have the list of factors with your additions to it, what do you do now? Consider each factor on its own. Assess each one without considering the others. For example, determine whether you are still interested in the industry. Maybe you have not wanted to be a sculptor for the past ten years. Maybe the stone and plaster is making you sick to your stomach. Think about that fact on its own.

The next thing to do is weigh each factor. Personally, I find being a lawyer to be very frustrating, but is my frustration alone enough to make me close up shop? Some factors will have enough weight on their own to make you quit the business. Buggy whip makers had to get out of business because the market shrunk to nothing. So the ones who weighed the industry's future did not have to consider other factors. The business was disappearing anyway. So, accept the fact that some factors alone can help you to determine if you should stay in business or get out.

Not all factors lead to the end result of quitting by the way. If your research and development firm invents a practical method for teleportation but you decide that you cannot stand working with your partner then that does not necessarily mean that you should get out. That teleportation stuff might actually make money. Maybe you should stay in at least for a while.

This brings me to perhaps the most important factor or aspect of the decision to stay or go. You need a plan. Some will say, "I only need a plan if I am quitting." You need a plan for both actually. Face it, if you are wrestling with the idea of closing your business, something has got to change. In the business context, change requires planning. If you are disappointed with sales forecasts and thinking of tossing it in but decide to stay, then you need a plan as to how to increase sales. If you are dissatisfied with the industry but you have no experience in any other business then you need to plan in order to spark your feelings for the industry. If you are quitting or staying, it should not matter. You need a plan.

So where does this "plan" come from? The best place to formulate a plan is from your list of factors to consider in whether you should stay open or close. The factors on the list usually open your mind to ideas as to how to implement your plan. This might sound complicated but it is not. Heck, even I could understand it.

Let us say that after considering everything, you realize that a major large company competitor is slashing prices in the industry to the point where you cannot go on. You simply have no profit margin left to compete.

You need some sort of exit strategy. More importantly, you need to determine how you are going to feed yourself. Or, if you are independently wealthy, you are going to need to figure out what to do with your time. At this point, pull out the list. Begin thinking about factors such as retirement and personal satisfaction. Your plan at this point should include a manner in which to retire and something that can bring you some level of satisfaction. Now consider if you enjoy the industry. If you do then you might develop a plan to sell your existing business to your competitor shifting the inventory and customer list to that competitor in exchange for an employment contract, benefits and the ability to take extended vacations.

Now let us try the other route. Let us say you decided to stay in your business because the long term forecast for the industry is very favorable. You are dissatisfied in the short term however. Nevertheless, you decide to stick it out until future prosperity presents itself. Pull out the list. Look at factors such as upcoming talent. Your plan should include training people to run the business for when it becomes more prosperous. Perhaps the enthusiasm from the new people entering your business will reignite your enthusiasm in the short run until such time that the business is so busy that you no longer have time to think about your personal satisfaction.

The list is a starting point. It is there to make you think. It is useful for brainstorming. The point is to use the list to assess whether you should stay or go and then, use the list to develop the plan for either route you choose.

CHAPTER 36
Am I Really on My Own?
Try a Little More Gratitude and a Little Less Attitude

One of the worst things a small business owner can do is become an island. You cannot be disconnected from everyone else in the world. Oh, I have met many small business owners in my time and a few have astounded me with comments like, "I am not much of a people person." I cannot possibly understand what would cause anyone operating their own business to say or think that. Let us be real. Until the time that computers are making the buying decisions for consumers and other businesses, the people running small businesses must be people persons. You really have no choice. People decide whether to buy what you have to sell. Therefore, it only makes sense that you, by necessity if not for any other reason, must interact with people.

Some will object, "that is what I have salespeople for." Yes but someone must interact with your salespeople. Some person hired them. It was probably you. The term management connotes interaction with people. If you are managing your own business then it is a certainty that you are dealing with others.

Now of course there will be days when you will feel a chip on your shoulder. You will feel that dealing with others is tedious and frustrating. You will seek the shelter of having only yourself to make happy. And you will feel justified for feeling that way. Indeed, there will be those days. The problem is that those days cannot last full days. You need to stop feeling like you want to get away from the rest of the world very soon after that feeling starts. That feeling becomes contagious. It spreads from you to your work force to your customers etc. It makes for poor communication. It sends the message that you are above dealing with people. It sends the message that people bother you. Soon, they will avoid you. You will suffer from loneliness and wither and die.

What caused the chip to be there? Why do we sometimes hate everyone else in the world? Why do we grow sick of dealing with other people and their problems? Why do we wish to become an island onto ourselves? Why do we develop some really bad feelings towards others?

It happens when we think more about ourselves than about others. It happens when we have more attitude than gratitude. Face it. If you somehow by the grace of God got the chance to open your own business then you probably owe somebody. There is a great probability that you owe a great many people. For instance, you owe the person or people who taught you the trade. You owe the people who taught you to read. You owe the people who taught you to talk. You owe the people who fed you when you had nothing. You owe to every customer who bothered to put faith in you or your products. You owe every teacher, friend and family member that ever cared about you. If I have inflicted sufficient guilt by now, you are probably thinking about a lot more people that you owe. If you are not feeling any guilt by this point then I am sorry but you are an ass. By the way, thanks for reading my book.

Now none of us likes to think about how we owe these people. Who wants to feel indebted to a mentor, or a parent, of a financier, or a friend, or a customer. Thinking about what we owe these people makes us feel bad about ourselves. So, rather than internalize that feeling, we push it outward. We resent the people that we owe. We feel justified standing head and shoulders above the crowd not remembering that we are standing on the shoulders of everyone who has ever helped us.

Retreating to an island does not show gratitude. It shows contempt. By retreating to an island, people indicate to the rest of the world that the world is bothering them. It sends a message to the world that the person has had enough of everyone else in the world and that despite owing others, the person just does not care. Off on your own island, the world cannot bother you and you cannot be bothered with the world.

The sad truth of the matter is that we see people like this all the time. Whereas they may feel sorry for themselves for having to deal with the rest of us, those of us not on the island pity them. There is nothing productive in their disdain for the rest of the world and the rest of the world sees no value to them.

People who are this disconnected, or seek to be this disconnected, lack the most essential aspect of what it takes to be in business for oneself. There is one element that everyone in business for themselves must have in order to be in business. It all comes down to proper perspective. My God we keep coming back to that word. Sorry. That word, or phrase, says it all. Proper perspective is what keeps you from being an island. That perspective is all about realizing the value of others.

How do we realize the value of others? Think about what other people mean to you. If you cannot do that, then think about what other people have done for you. If you cannot do that, then think about how you would feel if the people you need to appreciate were suddenly gone. Does their absence make you appreciate them? Does their absence make you realize their value? When they are gone, do things you need done get done? When they are gone, do you have everything that you need and want?

Proper perspective also requires that once you realize the value of others you show them your appreciation. Proper perspective means more than recognizing the value of others. It means that you appreciate and realize your obligation to show appreciation to others. Proper perspective is not merely about being grateful. It is also about showing gratitude.

What is at the heart of gratitude? Humility. Plain and simple, that is it. If you lack the capacity to be humble, you lack the ability to really make it in business. If you think that no one has helped you then you really have not properly and honestly assessed how you got to where you are. Once you can accept the fact that you owe what you have, and what you may have accomplished, to others, then you can erase those bad attitudes and feelings. You can overcome feeling like an island. More importantly, your humility will draw people to you. It opens the door for people to relate to you. When you are not head and shoulders above them, people can look you in the eye. When people can look you in the eye, they can feel comfortable with you. The comfort of your customers is the grease that will ease every transaction you will have with them.

If you have true humility then you will naturally feel the need to show appreciation. Humility is a feeling that has little value in and of itself unless it causes you to act a certain way. Humility differs from other feelings such as happiness. You can be happy for happiness sake. Humility is more like anger. It is worthless to be angry for anger's sake. The only true value to being angry is what the anger makes you do. The same is true for humility. For that reason, if you feel genuine humility, you will feel compelled to act on that humility. You will feel more than compelled. You will feel obligated to act.

The typical response to acting on one's humility is showing gratitude. This is the other part of having a proper perspective. When you feel the need to show your gratitude, then you have developed the requisite humility to be the type of person who can run a business. The reality of knowing that others have helped you and that you need to feel appreciation for them and to show appreciation to them is essential to the aspiring entrepreneur.

Demonstrating your gratitude through actions can take place in many ways and is not merely relegated to showing appreciation to customers. Perhaps you have a very good and loyal employee. Maybe the business would fold if you were to die. The kindest act of gratitude you could show to that employee is to think about what would happen to them if you died. Perhaps you should remember them in your will. Or, perhaps you should take out a small life insurance policy naming them as beneficiary if you die. Now, unless you really trust that person not to kill you to get the money, you really do not need to tell them about it. Your act of providing for them will remind you of what they mean to you and how grateful you are for their service. Besides that, it is something that you can throw in their face when they lose it one day and tell you that you do not appreciate them.

Now for those of you who feel that this is just too noble to be true and that it has little basis in the "real" business world, take note. Gratitude is a commodity. Doing things for others and showing appreciation makes people like doing business with you. When people feel that they want to do business with you, it translates to your bottom line. It is hard to quantify but it is there nevertheless. Your business will profit from you ability to be humble and show gratitude. It will be hard to establish a precise direct correlation but the business will benefit.

To prove this theory all you need to do is adopt a crappy attitude. Then, observe how long people will want to do business with you. Go back to thinking in terms of your little island. Develop a chip on your shoulder. Never say thank you to anyone and never say you appreciate anything. In fact, have no appreciation for anyone or anything. Act as though no one has ever helped you and even go so far as to act as if everyone owes you. Soon, you will observe your profits decline as employees will no longer want to work for you and customers will take their business elsewhere. So as you demonstrate your crappy attitude, you may not be able to gauge the precise amount that your profits will decline but they will decline nevertheless from the times when you demonstrate more humility.

People do not do business with people. People do business with attitudes. Customers and employees seek to do business with people who have a pleasant attitude. They want to do business with people who demonstrate humility and gratitude. Customers especially would like to think that their business is appreciated. In no less a manner, employees want to be appreciated for their work on behalf of your business. Vendors want you to appreciate what they do in order to serve you. All these parties want to feel as though their decision to do business with you as opposed to anyone else is appreciated by you. They want to feel as though they have value and significance to you.

How do they know you appreciate them? Your attitude tells them. Your attitude reflects the proper perspective we have been talking about. The attitude you display needs to be authentic. You cannot merely demonstrate a good attitude. Having a good attitude is not merely a matter of consciously deciding to have a good attitude. In order for the attitude to be authentic, it must be the result of you feeling genuine humility. Genuine humility will cause you to act in certain ways not the least of which will be actions demonstrating gratitude. This will generate the attitude that people seek in selecting with whom they want to do business.

So in making the various big decisions in operating your business, you should decide what attitude you want the business to illicit. You need to decide how you want to be perceived. If you are interested in the business's profitability and long term prosperity, then you should adopt a manner of thinking of yourself as not being alone on an island but rather as part of the world. As a part of the world, you can appreciate what others in the world do for you including giving you their business as opposed to taking it elsewhere. As you appreciate them, show them that you are humbled to have them choose you. Your humility should cause you to act to demonstrate your gratitude. Those actions of gratitude on your part will reinforce for them that they have chosen wisely in doing business with you. As they feel better about choosing you, you show more appreciation. That appreciation results in the customer looking to give you more business or the employee continuing with you. The cycle is established and it repeats.

The grease on the wheels of that cycle is your attitude. You cannot get that grease on an island.

CONCLUSION
My Kingdom for a Horse! For a Horse?

Richard III notwithstanding, your small business is a kingdom and you need to realize that you would not trade it for a horse. There may very well be days that you feel that you would trade it for substantially less than a horse but those are nothing more than random feelings of frustration. You are the person at the top of your business and that is valuable to you. It makes the business valuable to you in terms other than money. It is this feeling of being on top of your business that should cause you to realize that you are indeed, a king. Moreover, in the context of your business, you are THE king.

Come to grips with thinking of yourself as a king. Your small business is a kingdom. You have the authority over that kingdom. You have dominion over it. As you think about it, you ask yourself, "Am I a king?" Well, if you have more than one location for the business you own then you are not merely a king. Your multiple locations constitute an empire and therefore you are an emperor. The question to you then becomes, "am I a king or emperor of my business?" "Am I in command of this kingdom or empire?"

Being a king means that you set the policy of the kingdom. The rule of law in the kingdom is comprised of the legal proclamations of the king. The king establishes the rules of the kingdom. The king sets the goals of the kingdom. The king decides how resources will be used and distributed in the kingdom. The king decides what projects the kingdom will tackle and he decides the issues to be addressed and what issues can be ignored. The king sets the agenda for the kingdom. The king determines how the kingdom shall be run and how it should be perceived by the people in the kingdom and the people of other kingdoms. The king has sole authority to decide what the kingdom shall do. And the king usually plans how to use the resources of the kingdom to do his will.

Now much of what we just described should remind you of what you do for your business. You do all the same things for your business that the king does for his kingdom. You set policy and rules and determine the use of resources and establish how the business will be perceived and all the other things that the king does for his kingdom. It is no accident that the modern business model so closely reflects similar attributes to kingdoms. The concept of a kingdom is ingrained in us and the way we conduct our businesses naturally draws from this concept. The kingdom concept has lasted for centuries. We operate our businesses today in recognition of this very successful and durable form of management.

Just as a kingdom would be lost without its king, your business would be lost without you. Absent someone taking control and command over a kingdom, the kingdom does not function. Absent you taking control and command of your business, it would flounder and fade. So after recognizing the importance of you being able to serve as the king of your small business you can move onto the next question. "Am I a successful king? Has the kingdom prospered under my rule?"

To evaluate your performance as a king, think about what constitutes success for your kingdom. Once you have defined what factors are necessary for you to feel that the kingdom is successful, you need to think about how you measure that success. Typically, success is measured over time. Where was I yesterday, has my progress brought me any farther to day and can I be somewhere even better tomorrow? That is how we usually measure success. In business, the factor we customarily use to measure success is money and profit. These are the more traditional parameters we measure to determine the success of a business. People who are successful kings in their business are capable of maximizing profit and making money.

Some people seem to think that if you are a prosperous and successful business person then you probably lack morals, ethics or feelings. That just is not true and thinking of yourself like a king should not result in you adopting that way of thinking. Being the king does not mean that you are a ruthless dictator. Being a king does not necessarily mean that the power has gone to your head. A king can be benevolent. Even a king can have integrity. Kings can be wise and sensitive. The difference is that kings cannot be so sensitive as to usurp their own power out of a mere desire to be loved. Kings can care about their subjects but they do not care so much that they diminish their own power by giving their subjects authority over them.

When we use the terms "subjects" in our analogy we are not merely talking about employees and staff of a business. By "subjects" we mean all the assets of the business including staff, inventory, goodwill, customers, intellectual property, materials and cash and finances. Subjects constitute all that a king must consider in thinking about his kingdom and how to best utilize those subjects for the success of his kingdom. Just as in your business you do not merely manage your staff but you manage all the assets of your business in order to keep it moving forward, prospering and succeeding.

Kings are not equal to their subjects. A king has to preserve and enhance the kingdom. There is more responsibility for the king. Subjects merely need to preserve and enhance their own lives. Kings and subjects are not equal because the importance of what they must accomplish is not equal. Kings think in terms of kingdoms. Subjects think in terms of themselves. When you think about it this way, kings might even seem to have the more virtuous existence because kings have to think about everyone while subjects only need to think of themselves.

So when you think of yourself as the king of your business take heart. You must think in terms of advancing the kingdom not only for yourself but for your subjects. You must protect the kingdom and thereby, you must protect your subjects. You must make certain that your kingdom is treated fairly when dealing with other kingdoms. You must compete with other kingdoms and when the stakes of the competition are sufficiently high, you might even have to declare war. You must also make certain that your kingdom has a good reputation in dealing with other kingdoms. People from other kingdoms will seldom know anything about any individual subject but people will identify subjects with what they perceive about the kingdom they come from. How a king runs his kingdom will affect how people think about his subjects.

So for all the bad connotations that you might attribute to thinking about yourself as a king to your business, the analogy is still applicable. When you consider all the good things that a king must do and all the good things you must do, you start to feel better about being a king. You may start to feel that you are a better king than many others would be. You might feel that you have more heart than other kings and that maybe you are better to your subjects that other kings might be.

Then again, when you consider all the responsibilities that a king must endure, you realize that it will be difficult and often times frustrating to control, command and operate your kingdom. When you recognize that the king is ultimately accountable for his kingdom and that he is responsible for his subjects and that he will be blamed more often than he will be praised, being a king can be stressful. There might not be sufficient glory to justify it.

As these thoughts pervade your thinking, you will begin to realize that it will seem to be difficult more days than it might seem worth it. But, in the end, you need to ask yourself whether you really could work for anyone else. The answer to that is easy. When you realize that the success of your business is a reflection of your accomplishment as the one who leads it, it will occur to you. It's good to be the king.

www.ingramcontent.com/pod-product-compliance
Lightning Source LLC
Chambersburg PA
CBHW060838170526
45158CB00001B/182